# West Highland Terrier

## West Highland Terrier Training
### AAA AKC

### PAUL ALLEN PEARCE

# West Highland Terrier

## West Highland Terrier Training
### AAA AKC

**Think Like a Dog... but Don't Eat Your Poop!**

*Here's EXACTLY How to Train Your*

## West Highland Terrier

**PAUL ALLEN PEARCE**
P U B L I S H I N G

# What Our Customers Say – About Their Results!

**5.0 out of 5 Stars! | Five Stars!**

"I love my dog. I wanted to not only raise and train him, but understand his nature as well. With the help of this book, my dog are on the same page.

*- Vickie Lilly*

**5.0 out of 5 Stars! | Great Help With Our Rescue!**

"This book helped us to train the newly scared of his shadow 2yr old we recently rescued from an abusive home. I think he has a classic case of having a need to please. I'm happy to say he has come round to accepting our love & the rules our 12yr old follows"

*-Amazon Customer*

### 5.0 out of 5 Stars! | Awesome!

"Awesome book! Great for my dog and I"

- Michelle Dexter

### 5.0 out of 5 Stars! | Training!

"This book has helped me greatly. I recently adopted a 9 month old dog, named 'Ecko' after my dog passed away. I live in the country with a huge back yard and absolutely adore her. She is a wonderful addition." Thank you, Alison

-Alison

### 5.0 out of 5 Stars! | Five Stars!

"Easy instructions, well organized, and fun to read!"

-Vicki Cisneros

### 5.0 out of 5 Stars! | Puppy Training With a Sense of humor!

"Not only was this an easy read, it was humorous. I realized
that's the part I'm missing when training a pup - a sense of humor.
All steps were clearly outlined in addition to what to do
if the first attempts don't work out. This book was a great read
and very helpful."

- Pamela Cozart

### 5.0 out of 5 Stars! | Very Well Written & Entertaining

"Very well written and funny. Definitely speaks to the dog
owner. The only problem I can see is possible 'operator error'
lol."

-Jeanette Lucas

### 5.0 out of 5 Stars! | How Brilliant This Is

"This is a no nonsense, straightforward instructional training guide for you dog. Anyone who has ever had a puppy knows how brilliant dogs are. You need to understand how they think and react to kindness and challenges. A must for GSD but also an excellent guide for any dog owner."

- R. A. MOON

### 5.0 out of 5 Stars! | Excellent Resource of Information You Need To Know

"An excellent resource of information for to know my dog's history and for training him. It really works, and he teaches patience."

-Clarice B

### 5.0 out of 5 Stars! | Great Info

"I found the book very informative and a great guide to help me better understand my new puppy"

-D. Martillo

- ~ - ~ - ~ - - - ~ - ~ - ~ - 5 Star Reviews - ~ - ~ - ~ - ~ -- - ~ - ~ - ~ -

## 5.0 out of 5 Stars! | Great Info

"I have had three dogs, and this book was a great reference to go to when I needed help."

-Dotzee

- ~ - ~ - ~ - - - ~ - ~ - ~ - 5 Star Reviews - ~ - ~ - ~ - ~ -- - ~ - ~ - ~ -

## 5.0 out of 5 Stars! | Five Stars!

"Great small book, that echoes the advice and training of professional dog instructors. Good value.

-GDH

- ~ - ~ - ~ - - - ~ - ~ - ~ - 5 Star Reviews - ~ - ~ - ~ - ~ -- - ~ - ~ - ~ -

# Table of Contents

# New Dog Training Jump Start Guide

## *__Before__ You Just Go and Train*
## *Pick a Professional Trainer's Brain!*

**Learn Proven, Time-Saving Dog Training Success-Shortcuts**

# Introduction

Who is "man's best friend?" My wife says it's the couch, a pizza and ESPN, but that is because she grew up with four brothers. However, we all know man's best friend is his dog. I love my dog. I love dogs. They provide comfort, support, undying love, and someone to bounce all those brilliant ideas off that are going to make you a millionaire someday. I cannot imagine life without my dog.

When I picked Axel up and brought him home, he was a puppy. I was advised to train him well and not to make him a guard or an attack dog. Actually, training your dog makes him happier, healthier, and much more stable. Who knew?

With that in mind, I embarked on the journey of training this little puppy. Diving in head first, I bought books, acquired videos, and even talked with professional trainers about the matter. Over time, I gleaned a lot of helpful information. I learned about commonly encountered behavioral problems, and some not so common as well. I absorbed facts about proper diet, exercise, and training techniques. Because of my interest and commitment to his best interest, my dog is well behaved, happy, social, and understands a point spread better than any other dog traveling in the car pool lane.

While I was going through the process of learning how to train my puppy, I noticed one thing; *trainers are really, really,* serious about their craft, but will my lack of seriousness result in a poorly trained dog? The informality of my approach has resulted in a fabulous companion that clumsily bumps around the house, and chews on this and that in pure puppy form. Whether he's curled up snoozing or striking an adorable pose, the real joy comes simply from his mere presence, and of these joys, the laughter that he incites is at the very top of the list.

Keeping laughter and light heartedness in mind as a dog owner in training, is of the utmost importance because sometimes training can be very difficult on you and your pal. Sometimes your dog will push your patience to the limits. Remember to try and never let your dog know that you are at your limits. You are given the awesome responsibility at the time of acquisition, to be the pack leader and ultimately your dog's sensei.

I kept that in mind when I sat down to put this rewards based training book together. What I hope you will find inside here is a complete, concise training guide, the information of which is culled from trainers, training manuals and years of experience with a wonderful dog. Though this guide approaches training as a serious endeavor, your dog will teach you that it will not always be serious, and nor should you. I have attempted to infuse his playful spirit throughout this instructional. I hope that those light moments within this reading will help you get through the tougher times, like the chewing of your cell phone, the pooping on your socks and those mysterious expenses charged to your credit card. "Could it be that only Axel is able to run a credit card via telephone?"

A dog can be a loyal and longtime friend, worthy of your commitment and care. Your dog can give your life so much richness, and in return, asks very little. If you train your dog well, he or she will be happier, and as science has proven, so will you. If you keep a sense of humor alive during training, the outcomes will be the best for both of you. I hope you find this guide informative, easy to follow and fun. Enjoy.

# 1 The West Highland Terrier

## (Westie)

Westies have been around since the 1800's as the pets of English royalty and given as gifts to France. The Westie is considered the white offshoot of the Scottish and the Cairn terrier breeds. Originally bred to hunt rats, fox, badger, and other vermin, these highly energetic dogs are agile and like to stay very active.

I find that their independence and self-confidence make them good watchdogs, but in the annoyance category is their love for digging. Outdoors they are quick, wily, sporty, and good hunters, but indoors they are devoted and carefree. They have been called noisy and destructive but this can usually be controlled with proper socialization and obedience training. It is advised to be selective when finding a breeder and query about the temperament of their dogs.

The Westie may seem small, cute, and cuddly but they are not the type of dog that enjoys lounging upon laps for lengthy time, although this breed tends to be loyal and bond heartedly with their owners. In fact, they are said to be the most social of the Scottish terrier breeds and carry a strong zest for living.

Keep in mind that their hunting instinct cannot be trained away, but if they are raised with cats, they can learn to get along, but the same cannot be said for strange cats and other furry critters. When it comes to children, they usually do well and almost as well with strangers. The Westie temperament has been documented as varying and some may prefer solitude instead of playing with children. Keep an eye out for possessiveness, and again this can normally be handled with good socialization and training.

Intelligent, adaptable, spirited and durable, I know that you will find the Westie a terrific enthusiastic companion for all types of outings.

**History**

The history of dog breeds is often vague and a lot must be filled in until written records of a particular breed can be uncovered. The following is an often recited historical account of the West Highland Terrier. Like many terriers the Westie originated in Scotland where most of the terriers were dark in color. All of these terriers were used for hunting small game and controlling the rat, fox, otter, and various other vermin populations. Their method of hunting was to track, chase, and then if needed they would burrow into the ground and bolt their quarry. They were bred specifically for these tasks and their wiry hair was weatherproof to withstand the harsh Scottish climate. These short-legged terriers developed a rugged constitution and today they still maintain this attribute. It is unknown how long the different terriers roamed the Scottish Highlands before being recorded.

Distinct types developed in the different Scottish regions, many taking the name of the area that they were developed, such as the Cairn, and Scottish Terriers. The Scottish, Cairn, Skye, Dandie Dinmont, and West Highland terriers all hail from Scotland and originally all were grouped under the name Skye terrier.

In the late 1800's, the Malcolm family began breeding lighter Highland Terrier dogs that were light wheaten and white colored. The legend states this is due to the accidental death of one of his reddish terriers being mistaken for a fox, that henceforth he would only breed white terriers. Malcolm considered that the white terrier would be easier to find in the dense underbrush as well as easily distinguished between hunter and prey. It is stated that the Malcolm's developed their terriers for following game over stone and rock and thus they were required to be extremely agile and sure-footed. Others developed their terriers for burrowing purposes.

Firstly, they named their terriers Poltalloch or White Cairn stemming from the estate of the Malcolm family. Then others began developing their own strains of white terriers. In 1905, the White West Highland Club was formed and in 1906, the Kennel Club recognized the breed named the West Highland White Terrier. Soon after in nineteen hundred and nine, the West Highland White Terrier Club of America was formed and the breed was accepted into the American Kennel Club in 1908, under the name Roseneath Terrier, but in 1909, the name was officially changed to the West Highland White Terrier.

Today the Westie is still composed of their original character of confident, quick, wily hunters that enjoy digging and being active when outdoors. In 2016, the Westie is the 42$^{nd}$ most popular dog registered with the AKC.

**Health**

Like humans, dogs have the potential to develop ailments and diseases. Many of these ailments and diseases vary in type and prevalence, from breed to breed. Consider this fact when picking out your new puppy, and beware of any breeder that makes a claim that the puppies of their particular breed are *"100% healthy."* A reputable and honest breeder should know and share any health related issues that the breed you are purchasing or inquiring about might have, or that could potentially surface.

The possible health issues of the Westie; include luxating patella, Legg-Calve-Perthes disease, atopic dermatitis, juvenile cataracts, craniomandibular osteopathy, pulmonary fibrosis, aggression, and Addison's disease.

Westie Lung disease (idiopathic pulmonary fibrosis), which causes the connective tissues of the lungs to become inflamed and scarred causes breathing problems. This disease is believed to be genetic. Additionally white shake syndrome can develop between six months and three years and this condition causes trembling in afflicted dogs. They are also at a higher risk of developing bladder cancer. Not all of these conditions can be tested for detection.

Prior to acquiring your dog of choice, I recommend reading about canine health related issues and common breed specific ailments. By familiarizing yourself with the signs and symptoms of a potential disease or sickness, you will be empowered to be the first line of defense in support of your dog's health and wellbeing. By completing routine physical examinations of your dog, frequent fecal inspections, as well as recognizing any gastrointestinal problems, all helps to assure optimal health of your companion. By observing and understanding your dog's healthy behaviors and regular patterns, you will easily be able to identify when your dog is not feeling well, and to deduce if medical attention is needed.

In your position and role as alpha, you are responsible for providing the best possible care for your dog, assuring his or her wellbeing and comfort. Do not hesitate to consult your veterinarian if you observe your dog displaying peculiar behaviors or showing any signs of discomfort. It is very important to maintain your dog's scheduled exams, mandatory check up's and vaccination appointments. Uphold this duty, so that your dog can enjoy the vitality of good health that he or she deserves, and is entitled to.

Long daily walks are recommended for maintaining a healthy dog, regardless of the breed. Walks can be opportunities to practice leash training, socialization, and aid to the over-all mental and physical wellbeing of your dog. Westies will venture outside in any weather conditions so there is no need to think that your Westie will never want to go outdoors. Westies require at least an hour per day of varied types of exercise, whether this is achieved through play, games or sport. Tracking games are a great source of exercise and mental stimulation for Westies.

Remember that loneliness and boredom are enemies of the Westie. I advise that you always provide your new puppy with plenty of toys to keep boredom at bay and to reduce the chance of potential destructive negative behaviors from overtaking their disposition.

**Feeding Your West Highland Terrier**

Age, weight, and activity levels are a few of the factors that can change the food requirements of your Westie. Once you have determined the appropriate amount to provide, feed an accurately measured portion, at regular times, to help maintain their optimal weight. If you wish to feed your dog a raw food diet or a mix, please do your research and consult your veterinarian prior to any adjustments to their meals. Be sure to keep plenty of fresh, clean water available for your dog, and it is considered a good hygienic practice to clean your dog's bowl after each feeding.

More in "Nutrition"

**Proactive Measures for Puppy Selection**

If you want to buy a Westie puppy, be sure to find a reputable West Highland Terrier breeder who will provide proof of health clearances for both of the puppy's parents. Health clearances are official documents that prove a dog has been tested for, and cleared of any, or all breed specific conditions, however a clearance does not guarantee against acquired diseases or congenital abnormalities. Remember, even under the best breeding practices and proactive care measures, puppies can still develop diseases.

For the West Highland White Terrier breed, you should expect to see a health clearance from the Orthopedic Foundation for Animals (OFA) for patella and hip, as well as a clearance from the Canine Eye Registry Foundation (CERF), certifying that the eyes are healthy. You can also confirm health clearances by checking the OFA web site (offa.org). For more information, refer to the club website, breeder, or veterinarian. Consult the CHIC database for other tests and their schedules.

There are currently no screening tests for some of these conditions, including craniomandibular osteopathy; allergies and other serious skin conditions; Legg-Calve-Perthes disease; and copper hepatopathy which is a liver deficiency that allows elevated levels of copper to build up in the system.

The Orthopedic Foundation for Animals (OFA www.offa.org) maintains an open registry with evaluations of hips, elbows, eyes, thyroid, cardio, and additional canine health issues. They also provide clear definitions of the test categories to help you understand the grading system. PennHIP (www.pennhip.org) is another registry that tests and evaluates dog's hips.

The American Kennel Club (AKC) conducts large canine research studies on diseases that affect purebred dogs. Their health program is under the direction of the Canine Health Foundation (CHF), and is in partnership with OFA, and additionally does breed testing and provides a centralized canine health database called, the Canine Health Information Center (CHIC). The results of these tests are maintained in a registry, and dogs that have completed all of the required exams, including testing of the hips, elbows, and eyes, receive a CHIC number. Along with the breed-testing program, there is the CHIC DNA Repository. CHIC is trying to gather and store breed DNA samples for canine disease research. The goal is to facilitate future research aimed at reducing the incidence of inherited diseases in dogs. You can search the database to find out if a specific dog has information listed about it. More information about CHIC is available here: http://www.caninehealthinfo.org

To be accepted into the CHIC database, breeders must agree to have all test results published. This enables the reader to see both good and bad results of the testing. Obtaining a CHIC number does not imply that the dog received good or passing evaluation scores. The CHIC registration also does not signify as proof of the absence of disease, and all information must be read and evaluated. CHIC allows the information collected to be readily available to anyone with an inquiry.

## Care

You are responsible for the welfare of your new puppy or dog. Please treat him or her with respect and love, and this will be reciprocated tenfold. Dogs have been human companions for thousands of years, and they are living beings complete with feelings, emotions and the need for attachment. Before bringing home a new dog or puppy, please determine if you are capable and willing to provide all the needs that your new family member requires.

From the time you bring your pup home, positive training is a great start to introducing your new pack member to your household. You should be aware and sensitive to the fact that dogs have an amazing capacity for memory and recollection of those experiences. With this in mind, please refrain from harsh training tactics that may intimidate your puppy and that potentially can negatively affect personality or demeanor. When you train your new puppy, give him or her the respect they deserve, and utilize all available positive reinforcements. The result of your positive, proactive training methods and behavior modifications will be that your dog's abilities, traits, and characteristics that are buried within the genetic profile of their specific breed, will shine. I am an advocate for beginning with rewards based clicker training, followed by vocal and physical cues for your young dog to learn to become obedient to commands.

Crate training has positive benefits, and provides a safe place for your dog to nap, or simply to be alone. In addition, crate training at a young age will help your dog accept confinement if he ever needs to be transported, boarded or hospitalized.

Appropriate, early, and ongoing socialization will help you and your Westie throughout his or her lifetime. Expose your new puppy or dog to a wide variety of situations, people, and other animals. This helps to prevent shyness, aggressiveness, possessiveness, and many other potential behavioral problems, meanwhile supporting the bond between the two of you. Remember never leave young children unsupervised around dogs or puppies. Also, be aware that situations of aggression may happen no matter how loving, gentle, and well trained a dog may be.

A routine care program is essential for any dog, and should always include basic hygienic practices. For the optimal health of your pet, scheduled care should include the care of the coat, nails and teeth. It is important to get instruction from your veterinarian for the proper cleaning method of the outer and inner ear. The West Highland Terrier is white and has a harsh, straight haired double coat that sheds very little hair. The undercoat is soft and the outer, coarse, and easy to groom by daily using a stiff bristle brush. Their hair allows for dried mud and dirt to easily fall off or brushed away, so only bathe when necessary. Trim about every four months and strip twice yearly.

**Training**

Establish your alpha position and lead from there. Be consistent and firm in training and rule enforcement. They are tough little dogs full of energy so proper exercise helps to keep their barking and digging to a minimum. With their high prey drive, they will chase balls and devour toys. Never use yelling, jerking, and other physical punishment when training your Westie. These types of training can lead to many serious behavioral problems, such as fear, anxiety, and aggression. Continue training and socialization throughout their lifetime and offer plenty of rewards for positive behavior. They can sometimes be forceful and attempt to nudge you from your alpha position to get their way, so treat them as you would any dog, avoiding pampering just because they are so darn cute.

Pay special attention to training the commands, *leave it, come, stay,* and *leash* training. Their strong prey-drive makes it difficult to walk them off leash in any non-secure area. Giving chase to the neighborhood cats and all other potential furry targets is something that owners need to be acutely aware. Being struck by cars is common for all dogs with heightened prey drive and many a Westie has met their maker deciding to chase something. When Westies are in pursuit, they are single minded. They are known to housetrain quickly and enjoy their crates as their own safe haven. For the excavating Westie there is plenty of help in the "Digging" chapter.

Westies compete in a variety of sports, such as agility, Earthdog, Flyball, tracking, obedience, rally, tracking, coursing, conformation, and the new sport named Barn Hunt. This little terrier is indeed a gamer and enjoys being active and they are entertaining to watch and be around. A Westie owner should be able to properly exercise, train and regularly care for their dog or they will run into some negative behaviors.

To begin training, establish your *alpha position* from the moment you bring your new dog or puppy home. Leading as the alpha means that you are always consistent, calm, cool, and collected while enforcing rules and making corrections using a firm but fair attitude. The alpha always acts as though he or she knows that they are in charge.

The best time to begin training your puppy the basics is at around six weeks to eight weeks of age. Once your puppy realizes that you control schedules, toys, mealtimes and all the things he or she cherishes, he or she will respect you as the alpha in the family hierarchy. A positive step has been made when your puppy begins to follow you around the house. This means that he or she is bonding to you. Remember that all family members are above your dog in ranking, and it should remain that way.

Leading as the alpha assists you both in working together towards the goal of understanding the rules of conduct and obedience. Your dog will be at ease when the rules are understood. Put your puppy on a schedule for feeding, potty times, walks and play. Remain in control of toys and play time so that your Westie understands that you control all good things. This is important, because if your puppy doesn't have this structure early in life, he or she will grow up thinking that they can do as they wish. No matter how wonderful and easygoing your little Westie seems now, most likely that will change with age.

Gradually begin socializing your puppy from the time you bring him or her home. Proper early socialization that continues throughout your puppy's lifetime will provide you with a well-adjusted dog that is able to handle almost any situation in a calm manner. Early, thorough, and continual socialization is important for your West Highland Terrier. You do not want your dog being territorial and wary of strangers, so it is important to expose them early to a variety of situations, animals, people, and places. Socialization benefits you and your dog by providing you both with peace of mind.

With good socialization, you can expose your Westie to different situations with the assurance that he or she will look to you for guidance in rules of etiquette for the indoor and outdoor world. Socialization is the foundation for all well-adjusted dogs throughout their lifetimes.

Training a dog does not mean that your dog is supposed to only obey one master; they must learn to obey all commands given to them by the entire family and friend circle. In essence, when you are training, and learning to be a trainer, you also need to teach other family members and friends the correct way to issue these commands.

An effective incentive is to make everything you do seem fun. Always refrain from forcing your puppy to do anything they do not want to do. Highly prized treats are usually a great incentive to do something, and you will find that a fun, pleasant, friendly, happy, vocal tone combined with the treats will be ample reward for good behaviors and command compliance. Begin training all new commands indoors. This includes silencing all of your audio-visual devices that act as distractions to dog's sensitive ears.

Training should always be an enjoyable bonding time between you and your dog. Remember that all dogs are different, and that there is no set time limit for when your dog should learn, understand, and properly obey commands. Always have fun during training, remembering to keep your training sessions short, and stop if either of you are tired or distracted. I always suggest beginning training new tricks or commands in an area of least distraction. I promote starting with rewards based clicker training and ending with vocal and or physical cues for your dog to follow.

If you notice any negative behavioral issues, and are not quite sure if you are offering your dog proper socialization and necessary training, do not hesitate to enter your puppy into a puppy kindergarten class to assist you with training and socialization. Behavioral issues do not have to be present to enroll your dog into a puppy kindergarten; this assistance will benefit the both of you. Properly research the available classes so that their approach matches your own. The time to enroll your puppy is usually around eight to ten weeks of age, and after their first round of shots, although some kindergarten classes will not accept puppies until they are three to four months of age.

Reward good behaviors, but do not reward for being cute, sweet, loveable, or huggable. If you wish to reward your dog, always reward after you issue a command and your dog obeys the command. During your training sessions, be sure to mix it up, add a variety of toys and treats, and do not forget to have fun. Remember to provide them with ample daily exercise to keep them fit, healthy, and to keep behavioral problems at away. Provide consistent structure, firm authority, rule enforcement, love and affection, and you will have one heck of a dog for you and your family.

*Enjoy your West Highland Terrier dog!*

# 2 Socializing Your Westie

**What, Where, When, Why**

Everyone reads or hears socialization mentioned when researching about dogs. What is the reason for socialization? When is the best time to socialize a shiny new puppy? Does it have to do with getting along well with other dogs and people, or is there more to it? Do I let my puppy loose with other puppies, just sit back, and watch? These and many more questions are often asked, so let me provide the answers.

Dog socialization is for your dog to learn and maintain acceptable behaviors in any situation, especially when the dog or puppy does not want too. The goal is for your dog to learn how to interact with any normal experience that occurs in life without becoming overly stimulated, fearful, reactive or aggressive. No matter what the circumstance; your dog should be able to go with the flow, keep centered and remain calm. Proper socialization of your puppy is a crucial part of preparing him for the rest of his life.

Exposures to the many things we think are normal are not normal to our little puppies or adult dogs. Mechanical noises such as lawnmowers, car horns, blenders, coffee machines, dishwashers, stereos, televisions, garbage trucks, and other similar items make noises that dogs have to adjust too. Beyond mechanical noises are living creatures represented by other household pets, strange dogs, cats and critters in the yard such as gophers, rabbits, squirrels, and birds. Then dogs must become accustom to family members, friends, neighbors and of course the dreaded strangers.

All of the things mentioned above and more are new to most six-week-old puppies arriving at your house, so immediately begin the gradual introduction to these items and living creatures from arrival.

Continually remain alert to your puppy's reactions and willingness to either dive forward or withdrawal, and never force him or her to interact with things they do not wish too. Proceed at their pace by presenting the interaction and then observing their willingness of participation.

When strangers approach your pup do not allow them to automatically reach out and touch, leave a little space and time for your puppy's reaction to be observed, and then you can grant or deny permission based upon you and your puppy's intuition. We all know that many people fail to ask permission before reaching for dogs that are strange to them, so it is your job to instruct them in the proper interaction process.

**Socialization Summary Goals**

*- Learning to remain calm when the world is buzzing around them.*

*- Exposure in a safe manner to the environment that will encompass his or her world, including the rules and guidelines that accompany it.*

*- Learning to respond to commands when they do not want too. For example, in the midst of a tail chasing session with a fellow puppy, or while stalking an irresistible squirrel.*

Let us begin by looking at how a puppy's social development process is played out from puppy to adulthood.

The first phase of socialization begins as early as 3 weeks and lasts to approximately 12 weeks, during this time puppies discover that they are dogs and begin to play with their littermates. Survival techniques that they will use throughout their lives, such as biting, barking, chasing, and fighting, begin to be acted out.

Concurrently during this time-period, puppies experience big changes socially and physically. Learning submissive postures and taking corrections from their mother along with interactions with their littermates begin to teach them about hierarchies. Keeping mother and puppies together for at least 7 weeks tends to increase their ability to get along well with other dogs and learn more about themselves and the consequences of their actions, such as the force of a bite on their brothers and sisters.

Between the ages of 7-12 weeks, a period of rapid learning occurs and they learn what humans are, and whether to accept them as safe. This is a crucial period, and has the *greatest impact* on *all future social behavior*.

This is the time we begin teaching puppies the acceptable rules of conduct. Take note that they have a short attention span and physical limitations. This is the easiest period to get your puppy comfortable with new things, and the chance to thwart negative behavioral issues that can stem from improper or incomplete socialization.

The sad reality is that behavioral problems are the greatest threat to the owner-dog relationship and the number one cause of death to dogs under 3 years of age. It is your responsibility to mentor your dog so a problem does not arise, and that shouldn't be difficult because you adore your pup and enjoy being in his company.

From birth, puppies should be exposed to handling and manipulation of body parts, and exposure to different people, places, situations, and other well-socialized animals. Encourage your puppies exploring, curiosity and investigation of different environments. Games, toys, and a variety of surfaces and structures such as, rock, dirt, tile, concrete, pavement, tunnels and steps are all things to expose your puppy too. This exposure should continue into adulthood and beyond. This aids in keeping your dog sociable instead of shy, and capable of confronting different terrains.

Enrolling your puppy in classes before 3 months of age is an outstanding avenue to improving socialization, training and strengthening the bond between you and your puppy. You can begin socialization classes as early as 7-8 weeks. The recommendation is that your puppy has received at least *one* set of vaccines and a de-worming *seven* days prior to starting the first class. At his time, puppies are still not out of harm's way from all diseases, but the risk is relatively low because of primary vaccines, good care and mother's milk immunization.

It is important for your puppy to be comfortable playing, sleeping, or exploring alone. Schedule alone play with toys and solo naps in their crate or other safe areas that they enjoy. This teaches them to entertain themselves, and not become overly attached or have separation issues from their owners' absence. Getting them comfortable with their crate is also beneficial for travel and to use as their safe area.

Two phases of fear imprinting occur in your growing puppy's life. *A fear period is a stage during which your puppy may be more apt to perceive certain stimuli as threatening.*

During these two periods, any event your puppy thinks is traumatic can leave a lasting effect, possibly forever. The first period is from 8-11 weeks and the second is between 6-14 months of age. During these periods, you will want to keep your puppy clear of any frightening situations, but you will find that often difficult to determine. A simple item such as a chrome balloon on the floor could possibly scare the "bejeebers" out of your little pup. However, socialization continues and overcoming fears is part of that process so remain aware of what frightens your pup and work towards overcoming it.

There is no one-size-fits-all in knowing what your puppy finds fearful. Becoming familiar with canine body language can help you diagnose your pups fear factor. The second period often reflects the dog becoming more reactive or apprehensive about new things. Larger breeds sometimes have an extended second period.

Keep a few things in mind when seeking play dates for help with socializing your puppy. A stellar puppy class will have a safe mature dog for the puppies to learn boundaries and other behaviors. When making play dates, puppies should be matched by personality and play styles. Games such as retrieve or drop help to curb possessive behaviors as well as to help them learn to give up unsafe or off limits items so that the item can be taken out of harm's way. Another important lesson during play is for puppies to learn to come back to their human while engaged in a play session. *Your dog should be willingly dependent upon you and look to you for guidance.*

Teach mature easily stimulated dogs to relax before they are permitted to socialize with others. If you have an adult dog that enjoys flying solo, do not force him into situations. Teach your dogs and puppies less aroused play and encourage passive play. This includes play that does not encompass dominance, mouthing or biting other puppies.

If you have rough play happening between multiple dogs or puppies then interrupt the rough housing by frequently calling them to you and rewarding their attention. The attention then is turned to you. To dissuade mouthing contact, try to interject toys into the play. As they mature, elevated play can lead to aggression.

**The Importance of Play**

When observing dogs in a pack or family, one will notice that dogs and puppies often enjoy playing with each other. During play, puppies learn proper play etiquette, such as how hard to bite or mouth and the degree to play rough. Their mother and littermates provide feedback for them to learn. Play is instinctual and as an innate dog behavior is something that needs to be satisfied. Humans and dogs both play throughout their lifetime and many studies show that this social interaction is important for the mental and physical health of the individual.

Providing your dog with ample amounts of play through games, such as fetch, tug, or chase helps to satisfy their need for play, and assists in strengthening the bond between dog and owner. When guided in play, your dog will not only acquire the rules of play, but his physical and mental needs will be met during the activity.

One terrific bi-product of play is that it burns off excess energy and as a result, it helps keep negative behaviors from surfacing. Dogs are naturally full of energy and they need an outlet to avoid potential negative behaviors such as chewing, digging and barking. While these behaviors serve them well in the wild, when living with humans they can be a detriment to the harmony and success of the relationship.

**Socialization Summary**

- Proper socialization requires patience, kindness, and consistency during teaching. You and your dog should both be having fun during this process. Allow your dog to proceed into new situations at his or her own pace, never force them into a situation that they are not comfortable. If you think that your dog may have a socialization issue, seek professional advice from a qualified behavioral person. Do not delay because time is of the essence during their rapid growth period.

- During the first few months of socialization keep your puppy out of harm's way because he can easily pick up diseases from sniffing other dog's feces and urine. When you are first exposing your puppy to new people, places or cars, it is good practice to carry him to and from the car. Follow this practice both inside and outside when near dog clinics. Keeping your pup protected from contaminated ground surfaces will help keep him healthy until he has had vaccines and is a bit older. Avoid areas where you suspect other dogs might have eliminated.

- Socializing your puppy, especially before the age of six months, is a very important step in preventing future behavioral problems.

- Socializing can and should continue throughout the lifetime of your dog. Socializing in a gentle and kind manner prevents aggressive, fearful, and potential behaviors with possible litigious outcomes.

- A lack of socializing may lead to barking, shyness, destruction, territorialism, or hyperactivity, and the risk of *wearing Goth make up and the smoking of clove cigarettes*. The earlier you start socializing, the better. However, all puppies and dogs can gradually be brought into new and initially frightening situations, eventually learning to enjoy them. Canines can adapt to various and sometimes extreme situations, they just need your calm, guiding hand.

- If your puppy does not engage with other dogs for months or years at a time, you can expect his behavior to be different when he encounters them again. *I mean, how would you feel if your sixth grade math teacher who you haven't seen in 17 years, just walked up and sniffed you?*

- Meeting new kinds of people, including but not limited to people wearing hats, disabled folks, and people in local services such as postal carriers, fire and police officers, and crowds. *"Introducing your puppy to a circus clown is saved for another chapter."*

- Meeting new dogs is encouraged. Slowly expose your dog to other pets, such as cats, horses, birds, llamas, pigs, gerbils, and monitor lizards.

- Your dog's crate is not a jail. Be sure and take the time to teach your puppy to enjoy the comfort and privacy of his own crate. You want your dog's crate to be a place that he or she feels safe, for more information go to the crate-training chapter.

- To avoid doggy boredom, make sure your toy bin has plenty of toys for your puppy to choose. A Nylabone®, Kong® chew-toys, ropes, balls, and tugs are many of the popular things your dog can enjoy.

**Here are some methods you can use when exposing your dog to something new, or something he has previously been distrustful.**

- Remain calm and upbeat. If he has a leash on keep it loose.

- Gradually expose him to the new stimulus and if he is wary or fearful never use force. Let him retreat if he needs to.

- Reward your dog using treats; give him a good scratch or an energetic run for being calm and exploring new situations.

On a regular basis expose your dog to the things in the world that he should be capable of coping, basically everything. His gained familiarity will allow him to calmly deal with such situations in the future. Stay away from routine, such as walking the same route daily. Though dogs love routine, periodically expose your dog to new locations and situations. This allows you to assess his need for further socialization.

**Socialization Checklist for Puppies and Adult Dogs**

Be sure your dog is comfortable with the following:

- Male and female human adults.

- Male and female human children.

- Other household pets and dogs.

- Meeting strange dogs.

- Your house and neighborhood.

- Mechanical noises, such as lawn mowers and vehicles.

- Special circumstance people, for example, those in wheel chairs, crutches, and braces, Tourette syndrome or even strange indefinable *Uncle Larry*.

**To assure that your dog is not selfish, make sure that he or she is comfortable sharing the following:**

- His food bowl, toys, and bedding, and that they can all be touched by you and others.

- The immediate space shared with strangers, especially with children. This is necessary for your puppy's socialization so that he does not get paranoid or freak out in small places. For example, at the next-door neighbor's house or *Hollywood elevators filled with celebrities*.

- His best friend YOU, and all family members or friends, and is NOT overprotective or territorial towards others.

**For road tripping with your dog, make sure he or she is:**

- Comfortable in all types of vehicles such as a car, truck, minivan, and if applicable public transportation.

- Always properly restrained.

- You regularly stop for elimination breaks and hydration.

- *He knows how to operate a stick shift as well as an automatic.*

I have faith that you will do a terrific job in socializing your dog so that he can greet the world calmly and is able to enjoy the surprises it regularly delivers.

## ~ *Paws On – Paws Off* ~

# 3 "Well That's Not Good Behavior!"

**How to deal with a problem behavior before it becomes a habit**

Everyone likes his or her own space to feel comfortable, familiar, and safe. Your dog is no different. A proper living area is a key factor to avoiding all kinds of potential problems. Think of all the things your puppy will encounter in his life with humans, such as appliances and mechanical noises that are not common in nature, and can be frightening to your dog. It is essential to use treats, toys, and praise to assist you and your dog while in the midst of training and socializing.

Dogs are social creatures and it is essential to communicate with them. Communication is always the key to behavior reinforcement. Showing your dog that calm behavior is frequently rewarded, and that you have control over his favorite things, acts as a pathway to solving problems that may arise down the road.

Keep your dog's world happy. Make sure he is getting a proper amount of exercise and that he is being challenged mentally. Make sure he is getting enough time in the company of other dogs and other people. Keep a close eye on his diet, offering him good, healthy, dog-appropriate foods. Avoid excessive helpings when treating.

It is important that you be a strong leader. Dogs are pack animals and your dog needs to know that you are the *alpha*. Do not let situations fall into questionable scenarios that your dog is uncertain about who is in charge.

Your puppy will feel confident and strong if he works for his rewards and knows that he or she has a strong, confident leader to follow. Let your dog show you good behavior before you provide rewards. With a little work from him, he will appreciate it more.

Your dog's first step towards overcoming the challenges in life is in understanding what motivates his own behavior. Some behaviors your dog will exhibit are instinctual. Chewing, barking, digging, jumping, chasing, digging, and leash pulling are things that all dogs do because it is in their genetic make-up. These natural behaviors differ from the ones we have inadvertently trained into the domestic canine. Behaviors such as nudging our hands asking to be petted, or barking for attention, are actually accidently reinforced by us humans and not innate.

What motivates your dog to do what he does or does not do? You may wonder why he does not come when you call him while he is playing with other dogs. Simply, this may be because coming to you is far less exciting than scrapping with the same species. When calling your dog you can change this behavior by offering him a highly coveted treat and after treating, allow him to continue playing for a while. Start this training aspect slowly, and in short distances from where he is playing. Gradually increase the distances and distractions when you beckon your dog. After he is coming regularly to you then begin to diminish the frequency of treating, and supplement verbal or physical praise.

**Here are some helpful tips to use when trying to help your West Highland Terrier through challenging behavior.**

- Are you accidentally rewarding bad behavior? Remember that your dog may see any response from you as a reward. You can ignore the misbehavior if you are patient enough, or you can give your puppy the equivalent of a human *time out* for a few minutes. Make sure the time out environment is in a calm, quiet and safe, but very dull place that is not his crate.

- Think about the quality of his diet and health. Is your dog getting enough playtime, mental and physical exercise, and sleep? Is this a medical problem? Do not ignore the range of possibilities that could be eliciting your dog's challenging behavior.

- Be sure and practice replacement behavior. Reward him with something that is much more appealing than the perceived reward that he is getting when he is acting in an undesirable manner. It is important to reward his good behavior before he misbehaves. If done consistently and correctly, this will reinforce good behaviors, and reduce poor behaviors.

For example, in the hopes of receiving love, your dog is repeatedly nudging your hand; teach him to *sit* instead by only giving him love after he sits, and never if he nudges you. If you command, "sit" and he complies, and then you pat him on the head or speak nicely to him, or both, your dog will associate the sitting compliance with nice things. If he nudges and you turn away and never acknowledge him he will understand that behavior is not associated with nice things. In a scenario where your dog is continually nudging you for attention, catch him before he comes running into your room and begins nudging. When you see him approaching, immediately say, "sit" to stop him in his tracks.

- While practicing the replacement behavior, be sure you reward the right response and ignore the mistakes. Remember, any response to the wrong action could be mistaken as a reward by your dog, so try to remain neutral in a state of ignoring, this includes, sight, touch and verbal acknowledgement. Be sure to offer your dog a greater reward for the correct action than the joy he is getting from doing the wrong action.

- Your dog's bad behavior may be caused by something that causes him fear. If you decipher this as the problem, then change his mind about what he perceives frightening. Pair the scary thing with something he loves. For example, your dog has a problem with the local skateboarder. Pair the skateboarder's visit with a delicious treat and lots of attention. He will soon look forward to the daily arrival of the skateboarder.

- Always, remain patient with your dog and do not force changes. Work gradually and slowly. Forcing behavioral changes on your dog may lead to making the behaviors worse. Training requires that you work as hard as your dog, and maybe harder, because you have to hone your observational skills, intuition, timing, patience, laughter, and the understanding of your dog's body language and demeanor.

## ~ *Paws On – Paws Off* ~

# 4 Effective White Terrier Training

I often find them easy train, but they often show their stubbornness and decide not to obey. This might seem confusing, so let me clarify. They are generally quick and intelligent learners but their will to do their own thing overpowers what we want and expect. The implication here is that they have learned the command words and know what is expected but might not comply as often as owners would like. You should always be training when around your dog, so use those opportunities to ask for an action and always reward with praise or play.

After all, they are terriers and it is in their nature to think and act independently. You may find that you need extra repetitions and continual practice sessions to keep your Westie tuned to obey your instructions. Don't fret; it is part of Westie ownership. These characters are true terriers, and with that come independence, stubbornness and willfulness.

Now, I am sure that there might be a few Westie owners beside themselves right now with because their little white dogs are super obedient sweethearts that love cuddling and never tear anything up. I will agree that there might be a few mellow Westies out there; after all, they all have their own unique quirks and dispositions.

Knowing what you want to train your Westie to do is as important as training your dog. You can begin training almost immediately, at around six weeks of age. A puppy is a blank slate and does not know any rules, therefore it is a wise idea to make a list and have an understanding of how you would like your puppy to behave.

What are the household rules and proper dog etiquette? As he grows, the same principle applies and you may adjust training from the basics to more specialized behaviors, such as making your dog a good travel, hiking, agility, hunting, or simply a companion dog. Know what conditions and circumstances you plan to expose your dog or puppy to outside of the household and strategize to be prepared for those encounters by slowly introducing your dog to those situations.

Establish yourself as the pack leader from the time you first bring your new dog or puppy home. Being the alpha assists in the training process, and your dog's relationship with you and your family. Life is much easier for your dog if you are in charge, leading, and providing for his needs.

Leading as the alpha assists in the act of working together with your dog towards the goal of understanding the rules of conduct and obedience. Your dog will be at ease when the rules are understood. Training should be an enjoyable bonding time between you and your dog.

Remember that there is no set time limit defining when your dog should learn, retain, and then obey commands. Use short training sessions and be aware that if either of you are tired, it is recommended that you stop and try again later. If something does not seem quite right with your dog, in any way, have him checked out by a veterinarian.

- *Timing is crucial* when rewarding for good behaviors and making corrections for bad.

- *Patience* and *Consistency* are your allies in the training game.

An easy way to avoid the onset of many different behavioral problems is to give your dog's ample daily exercise to keep them fit healthy and keep destructive behavioral problems at bay. Always provide consistent structure, firm but fair authority, rule enforcement, and importantly, love and affection. By maintaining these things, you will help to create a loyal companion and friend. Reward good behaviors but not simply for being cute, sweet, loveable, and huggable. If you wish to reward your dog, always reward after you issue a command and your dog obeys appropriately.

- Only train one command per session. Puppies and many breeds only have the attention span to go about 5 - 10 minutes per session, but never exceed 15 minutes. Training a command once per day is enough for your dog to begin to learn and retain. It is easy to perform at least 3-5 training sessions in a day, but whenever the opportunity presents itself you should reinforce the training sessions throughout the day.

For example, when opening a door or putting down a food bowl, first command sit, down or stay and be sure not to reward your dog unless your dog obeys. The most important thing to remember is to remain relaxed, keep it fun, and enjoy this time of bonding and training your puppy.

Five to ten minutes per session is a good time limit for young puppies. Some breeds remain puppies longer than others remain and may not fully develop until year two, however as they mature many dogs will begin to remain focused for longer periods. Use a variety and an abundance of different treats and rewards. Rewards are play, toys, praise, affection, treats, and anything that you know that your dog enjoys.

- All dogs have their own personalities and therefore respond to training differently. You need to account for individual personality and adjust accordingly. If needed, do not hesitate to solicit professional help and advice.

- We all love treats, and so does your dog. Giving your dog a treat is the best way to reinforce good behavior, to help change his behavior or just to make your dog do that insanely funny dance- like-thing he does. Make the treats small enough for him to get a taste, but not a meal, kernel sized. Remember, you do not want him filling up on treats as it might spoil his dinner and interfere with his attention span, and large treats take time to chew and swallow, thus interrupting the session.

- Keep a container of treats handy with you at all times. You do not want to miss a chance to reward a good behavior or reinforce a changed behavior. Always carry treats when you go on a walk.

Remember what treats your dog likes most and save those for special times, like the big break-through. In addition, what you consider a treat and what your dog considers a treat are two vastly different worlds. A single malt scotch or chicken wings might be a treat in your mind, but dried liver bits or beef jerky in your dogs.

- Ask for something before you give the treat. Tell your dog to sit, stay, or lie down, print two copies of your resume, anything, before you reward your dog with treats, petting, or play. By asking for good behavior, before you give your dog a reward, you demonstrate you are in charge, in an easy fun manner.

There is a common misconception that dogs are selfless and wanting to behave only to please out of respect for you. This is horse pucky. This line of thinking is incorrect and detrimental to your success with the training. You have to make sure that your dog knows exactly why he should be listening to you, and exactly what action you want from him. You are the alpha, the keeper of the treats, the provider of the scratching and the purveyor of toys. Keep this balance of power and the results will be your reward.

- Be positive. Think about what you want your dog to do, instead of what you don't want him to do. Do not send mixed messages. Simply, ignore the bad behaviors and reward your dog when he does the action you request. Begin with the basics each your dog some simple commands to communicate what you want, such as, Sit, Come, and Stay, Drop it, and Leave it.

- Regular vigorous exercise! It is understood that your dog will be much happier if you run your dog every day. Run your dog until his tongue is hanging out. If he is still full of energy, run him again and he will love you for this and sleep better at night. There will be times that before a training session begins you will need to use a little exercise to release some of your dog's energy; this can increase his ability to focus during the session. Toy and many small dogs do not require excessive exercise but still require daily walks and play sessions.

- It is very important that you make sure your dog is comfortable in all sorts of situations. All dogs, even your sweet tempered Pup, have the potential to bite. Making sure, he is comfortable in various situations and teaching your dog to be gentle with his mouth will reduce the risk of unwanted bites. Mouthing should not be acceptable behavior because it leads to potentially harmful actions.

- Kids are great, are they not? However, the notion that kids and dogs are as natural a pairing as chocolate and peanut butter is simply not true. Kids are often bitten by dogs because they unintentionally do things that frighten dogs. Sometimes a child's behavior appears like prey to a dog.

Never leave a dog and a child together unsupervised, even if the dog is good with children. Teach children not to approach dogs that are unfamiliar to them. The way a child behaves with the familiar family dog may not be appropriate with another dog that they meet for the first time. Instruct children that tail pulling, hugging their necks tightly, leg pulling, and hard head pats are unacceptable.

There exists many different ways to train puppies. Using clicker and rewards based training is an effective and humane way to train dogs and treat them with kindness.

Lying ahead of you will be the task of navigating your dog's unique personality, which will affect your training and relationship. Although, you have no doubt read and watched much about training, spoken with friends and breeders, your dog's personality is why it is imperative to keep an open mind and use your intuition to guide you while training, be flexible.

Your consent as the owner is the one thing that will allow your dog to become disobedient, out of control, and possibly a danger to your family and the outside world.

Arming yourself with knowledge about dog behaviors, and understanding your own dog's personality will greatly assist you throughout the process of training and companionship alongside your dog. It is your responsibility to guide and train your dog to be a socially adjusted obedient dog so that the two of you have a fruitful relationship. Well-behaved dogs are welcomed anywhere and your goal should be to train your dog to be well behaved and obedient.

## Terrier Breeds Traits

All dogs come with their own unique individual personalities, but they also carry forward their heredity. Having knowledge of the original breeding purpose, where traits were both bred in and out, helps to offer insight into the characteristics of your particular breed. Those negative and positive behaviors that you might encounter as you are raising, training, and living with your new dog are directly linked to intentional trait manipulation.

I am including information on *terrier breeds* to offer you the owner and trainer further insight into the character these types of dog carry with them from their pedigree. The more information known about your Westie, the better you will be equipped to train.

Many terrier dog breeds were developed in the United Kingdom with a common and practical focus of locating and killing vermin. Needing to fit into rodent burrows, most terriers tend to be small and lean with a rough wiry coat that requires little maintenance. In addition to their job as rodent exterminators, they were bred for foxhunting, sport, and dog fighting. A result of this specialized breeding, terriers were often pugnacious and aggressive, but over subsequent years, most of these traits have been greatly reduced throughout many of the terrier breeds. Numerous terrier breeds are quite vocal and are inclined to chase moving objects. They also have a fearless demeanor that keeps them from retreating during confrontations.

Many terrier breeds are named from the area in which that particular breed was developed, for example, Norwich, Bedlington, Irish, Border, Patterdale, Skye, West Highland and Boston. Depending upon by who and how they are categorized, there an estimated sixty to one-hundred terrier breeds.

Generally, hunting terriers have a low tolerance for other animals, including other dogs. Since terriers were originally bred to hunt, chase, and kill rodents, otters, fox and other animals, their independence and predatory drive persists. This is one of the reasons why these terrier breeds love to dig, because they are used to pursuing and dispatching their prey, often when underground. This residual predatory drive is why furry pets, including cats, will always be in danger of chase and possible attack. Of course, the larger Bull Terriers were not bred to chase prey and hunt but instead for sports such as bull baiting and sport fighting.

Most terriers have a fearless streak, which often makes them willing and ready to confront other animals and if necessary, humans. Usually friendly and enjoying human company, terriers are often reserved around strangers. Terriers are generally not the type of breed that is glued to their humans, perpetually under foot. However, when they decide to show affection most are warm and affectionate towards their owners. As for fur, many of the terrier breeds carry a wiry coat that requires a grooming technique named stripping to keep the color and fur in proper condition. Stripping pulls the shed hair from the coat and maintains the dogs distinguishing coat texture and color. Others carry a short flat lying easy to groom coat.

With their representative spunk, energy, and stubbornness, owning a terrier normally requires owners to be strong willed and able to maintain, as well as assert their alpha dominance. This essential role of pack leader can only be achieved and maintained through consistent reinforcement, discipline and ongoing training. It should be noted that not all terriers get along with other dogs, and in general are often considered best suited to be the only family dog.

Because of their high energy and playfulness, terriers make terrific pets if they are properly socialized. Through early socialization, most terriers will get along well with other dogs, and sometimes with cats. It is important to begin training your terrier puppy at around six to eight weeks, and ongoing throughout their lifetime. Do not forget to provide daily vigorous exercise for your energetic terrier. An absence of exercise often leads to various negative behavioral and health issues, which can manifest in highly unwanted and destructive behaviors.

Digging and barking can be troublesome with terriers, so it is suggested to correct these issues early using ongoing behavioral modifications and training your terrier that a couple of warning barks are all that is necessary. A serious digger can prevent you from having a productive garden or a nice plot of lawn, and incessant barking will not only disturb your peace, but that of your neighbors. For digging help, you may consider creating a special area, such as a designated digging pit for them to do what they do best. For the canine escape artist, and terriers are masters, proper fencing that extends down into the ground about one foot (30cm), or chicken wire buried deep beneath the soil will help to prevent the potential for a breach.

A talented breed, terriers compete in sports of agility, including lure racing, Frisbee™, and flyball. They are also excellent at scenting, Earthdog trials, which tests their skills as hunters without prey. Terriers are quick and athletic, and often enjoy accompanying humans while hiking, jogging, or during long walks. They require strong, consistent leadership, and usually respond well to rewards based clicker training. Remember to expect that many of the terrier's strong characteristics will challenge your spot as the alpha leader, so it is essential to remain diligent in securing and maintaining the role as your dog's leader and provider, which sums up to being an active participant in your terriers life while providing for their needs.

Reinforce wanted behaviors with frequent rewards, such as treats, play, and praise. As a part of their breeding, terriers are independent and accustomed to solving problems on their own, so incentives will help you in training. The commands *stay*, *come*, *leave it* and *no*, should be taught early and practiced regularly.

**Terrier Types & Groups**

Breed group classifications are not scientific and vary within the different kennel clubs. For example, the Miniature Schnauzer is placed in the Terrier Group by the American Kennel Club but not categorized as Terrier by the Kennel Club (UK), which places all Schnauzers in the Utility Group. Boston Terriers are true terriers although the Kennel Club also places them in the Utility Group, while the Canadian Kennel Club places them in the Non-Sporting Group. The Tibetan Terrier is not a true terrier, and thus only a terrier by name. No matter which group the different terriers are classified, a terrier is still a terrier. In 18th century Britain, terriers were divided into two groups, long and short-legged. Just keep in mind terrier categorization is informal and non-scientific.

## Working Terriers

These hunting type terriers are still used to find, track, trail, and hold prey at bay. Many specialize in underground type hunting where they attempt to bolt the prey into the hunter's sights. Some of these are the Jack Russell, Patterdale, Cairn, Scottish, and West Highland White Terrier. All of these types were originally bred and trained to hunt and kill small vermin in barns, homes, and around farms, and if necessary go underground to bolt or kill the prey.

## Fell Terriers

These terriers were developed in Northern England and their primary focus was to assist hunters in killing foxes by either bolting the fox from its den or killing it by itself. They are long legged working terriers such as the Patterdale, Lakeland, and Black Fell Terrier, usually weighing less than 15lb (6.5kg), and having narrow chests that enable them to fit into burrow entrances. They are bred strictly for hunting ability and gameness.

## Hunting Terriers

These terriers were developed in Southern England and their primary focus was to assist hunters in locating and bolting foxes during traditional mounted foxhunts. Horse oriented social clubs chasing red fox utilize these types of terrier breeds. Some breeds that came from these are the Jack Russell, Plummer, Toy Fox, Fox, and the Brazilian Terriers.

## Toy Terriers

These types of terriers were bred down in size from larger terriers with the primary focus of companionship and showing in the Toy category. The Toy Fox, Manchester, Russian Toy, and the Rat Terriers are a few in this category. Although small in stature, they are still terriers in personality and do not enjoy lazing around on their masters laps in the manner true companion dogs often enjoy. Toy terriers retain a strong predatory drive, during hunting they would be carried upon horseback, and released once the prey was near.

## Bull type Terriers

These dogs came from crossing Bulldogs and terriers and their original purpose was for sports such as bull baiting, bear baiting, and pit fighting, as well as being used for guarding purposes. As these practices grew out of favor and laws were passed prohibiting these activities, breeders began to make these bull type dogs into easy-going, highly trainable family dogs that could be trusted with children and other animals.

Unfortunately, the underground fighting of these dogs has continued and thrived. This has contributed to an unearned stigma that has grown into anti-bull legislation and demonization of these breeds, such as the American Pit Bull, Bull Terrier, Staffordshire Bull Terrier, and American Staffordshire Terrier. The media has unfairly contributed to this with their sensationalist and often-incorrect coverage of dog attacks. The onus lies with us humans in the mistreatment of these dogs, and with the purposeful breeding of aggressive traits simply to continue with the blood sport of pit dog fighting. These aggressive traits were successfully bred out of these breeds, for example the Staffordshire Terrier, who continues to be a beloved family dog that is affectionate, good with children and a trustworthy dog to have in the house without concern for aggression.

I hope this brief historical over-view has provided some extra insight into your terrier, especially those hunting terriers and the motivation behind their actions of chasing, digging, and boundless energy.

## ~ *Paws On – Paws Off* ~

# 5 Rewards not Punishment

It is always better to reward your Westie instead of punishing him or her. Here are a few reasons why:

- If you punish your dog, it can make him distrust, or cause fear, aggression, and avoidance of you. If you rub your dog's nose his doodie or pee, he may avoid going to the bathroom in front of you. This is going to make his public life difficult.

- Physical punishment has the tendency to escalate in severity. If you get your dog's attention by a light tap on the nose, he will soon get used to that and ignore it. Shortly the contact will become more and more violent. As we know, violence is *not* the answer.

- Punishing your dog may have some bad side effects. For example, if you are using a pinch collar, it may tighten when he encounters other dogs. Dogs are very smart, but they are not always logical. When your dog encounters another dog, the pinching of the collar may lead him to think that the other dog is the reason for the pinch. *Pinch collars have been linked to the reinforcement of aggressive behaviors between dogs.*

- Electric fences will make him avoid the yard.

- Choke collars can cause injuries to a dog's throat as well as cause back and neck misalignment.

- You may inadvertently develop and adversarial relationship with your dog if you punish your dog instead of working through a reward system and correctly leading. If you only look for the mistakes within your dog, this is all you will begin to see. In your mind, you will see a problem dog. In your dog's mind, he will see anger and distrust.

- You ultimately want to shape your dog's incorrect actions into acceptable actions. By punishing your dog, he will learn only to *avoid* punishment. He is not learning to change the behavior you want changed, instead he learns to be sneaky or to do the very minimum to avoid being punished. Your dog can become withdrawn and seemingly inactive. Permanent psychological damage can be done if a dog lives in fear of punishment.

- If you punish rather than reward neither you nor your dog will be having a very good time. It will be a constant, sometimes painful struggle. If you have children, they will not be able to participate in a punishment based training process because it is too difficult, and truly no fun.

- Simply put, if you train your dog using rewards, you and your dog will have a much better time and relationship. Rely on rewards to change his behavior by using treats, toys, playing, petting, affection, or anything else you know your dog likes. If your dog is doing something that you do not like, replace the habit with another by teaching your dog to do something different, and then reward him or her for doing the replacement action, and then you can all enjoy the outcome.

## ~ *Paws On – Paws Off* ~

# 6  Clicker Training Your Westie

What the heck is that clicking noise? Well, it's a clicker, thus the name. If

you are a product of a Catholic school, you might be very familiar with this device. You probably have nightmares of large, penguin like women clicking their way through your young life. Yes, it was annoying and at times, terrifying, however, when it comes to training your dog, it will be helpful and fun.

A clicker is a small device that makes a sound that is easily distinguished and not common as a sound in nature, or one that humans normally produce. This unique sound keeps the dog that is being trained from becoming confused by accidently hearing a word used in conversation or another environmental noise. You click at the exact time when your dog does the correct action then immediately follow the click with a treat or reward.

The clicker is used to inform your dog that he did the right thing and that a treat is coming. When your dog does the right thing after you command, like drop your Chanel purse that is dangling from his mouth, you click and reward him with a nice treat. Using the clicker system allows you to set your puppy up to succeed while you ignore or make efforts to prevent bad behavior. It is a very positive, humane system, and punishment is *not* part of the process.

**Here are some questions often asked about the clicker training:**

- "Do you need to have the clicker on your person at all times?" *No.* The clicker is a teaching device. Once your dog understands what you want your dog to do, you can then utilize a verbal or hand cue, and if inclined verbal praise or affection.

- "Can rewards be other things besides treats?" *Sure.* Actually, you should mix it up. Use the clicker and a treat when you first start teaching. When your puppy has learned the behavior you want, then switch to other rewards, such as, petting, play, toys, or lottery tickets. Remember always to ask for the wanted target behavior, such as, *sit, stay,* or *come,* before you reward your dog. These verbal reinforcements can augment the clicker training and reward giving.

- "With all these treats, isn't my dog going to get fat?" *No.* If you figure treats into your dog's daily intake and subtract from meals accordingly, your dog will be fine. The treats should be as small as a corn kernel, just a taste. Use food from his regular meals when you are training indoors, but when outdoors, use fresh treats like meat or cheese. There are many distractions outside and a tasty fresh treat will help keep your puppy's attention. Dog's finally honed senses will smell even the smallest of treat, and this keeps them attentive. -"What do I do if my dog doesn't act out the command?" *Simpl*e, if your dog disobeys you, it is because he has not been properly trained yet. Do not C/T (Click and Treat), or verbally praise for any wrong actions, ignore the wrong action. Continue training because your dog has not yet learned the command and action you are teaching him to perform. He, after all, is just a dog. If he is disobeying, he has been improperly or incompletely trained, maybe the treats are not tasty enough. Try simplifying the task and attempt to make the reward equal to, or better than what is distracting your dog. Eventually your dog will understand what action should be performed when the command word is spoken.

**HELPFUL HINT**

- *Conceal the treat! Do NOT* show your dog the treat before pressing the clicker and making the clicking sound. If you do this, he will be responding to the treat and not the click and this will *undermine* your training strategy.

# Why and How Clicker Training Works

The important reason I put this information together is that it is essential to understand why timing and consistency is important, and why clicker training works. If any of this is confusing, do not worry, because I walk you through the training process, step-by-step.

Clicker training started over seventy years ago and has become a tried and true method for training dogs and other animals. The outcome of using a clicker is an example of conditioned reinforcement. Rewarding the animal in combination with clicker use has proven highly effective as a positive reinforcement training method. It is a humane and effective way of training dogs without instilling fear for non-compliance. I know that my mother wished she would have known about clicker training when my brother and I were growing up. I am sure she would have put the clicker into action so my brother would place his dirty clothes inside the bin, rather than on the floor.

In the 1950s, Keller Breland, a pioneer in animal training, used a clicker while training many different species of animals, including marine mammals. He met great success using this method of training on these animals. His system developed for clicker training marine mammals is still in use today. Keller also trained dogs using the clicker. Because of its effectiveness, it was brought into use by others in the dog training community. Gradually, clicker training for dogs gained more and more popularity and by the early 1980's its use became widespread. The success of the clicker spans 7 decades and now is a widely accepted standard for dog training.

A trainer will use the clicker to mark desired actions as they occur. At the exact instant, the animal performs the desired action, the trainer clicks and promptly delivers a food reward or other reinforcements. One key to clicker training is the trainer's timing, as *timing is crucial*. For example, clicking and rewarding slightly too early or too late will reinforce the action that is occurring at that very instant rather than the action you were targeting the reward for. The saying goes, "you get what you click for."

Clicker trainers often use the process of *shaping*. Shaping is the process of gradual transformation of a specific action into the desired action by rewarding each successive progression towards the desired action. This is done by gradually molding or training the dog to perform a specific response by first, reinforcing the small, successive responses that are similar to the desired response, instead of waiting for the perfect completion to occur. The trainer looks for small progressions that are heading in the direction towards the total completion of the desired action and then clicks and treats. It is important to recognize and reward those tiny steps made in the target direction. During training, the objective is to create opportunities for your dog to earn frequent rewards. In the beginning, it is acceptable to increase the frequency of a C/T to every 3-4 seconds, or less. By gauging the dog's abilities and improvements, the trainer can gradually increase the length of time between C/T. It is necessary to assess the dog's progress from moment to moment, adjusting C/T to achieve the desired actionable outcome.

During training, and in conjunction with clicker use, the introduction of a cue word or hand signal can be applied. Eventually, the clicker can be phased out in favor of a cue or cues that have been reinforced during the training sessions. As a result, your dog will immediately respond by reacting, obeying, and performing actions to your hand gestures or verbal commands. Watching this unfold is a highly satisfying process, which empowers your friend to be the best he can, and while you have fulfilled your role as *alpha* and pack leader.

**Why is clicking effective over using a word cue first?**

The clicking sound is a unique sound that is not found in nature, and it is more precise than a verbal command. Verbal commands can be confusing because the human voice has many tonal variations, whereas the clicker consistently makes a sound that your dog will not confuse with any other noise. It is also effective because it is directed at him and followed by good things. Therefore, your dog completely understands which action is desired and your dog will quickly understand that the click is followed by a reward.

The clicker sound is produced in a quick and accurate way that is in response to the slightest actions that your dog makes. This clarity of function of this tool increases the bond between you and your dog, as a result making your dog more interested in the training sessions, and ultimately your relationship more engaging and entertaining. Dare I say fun? On that note, do not forget to always have fun and add variety to your training sessions. Variety is the spice of life, mix up those treats, rewards, and commands.

**Clicker training works this way**

At the *exact* instant the action occurs, the trainer clicks. If a dog begins to *sit*, the trainer recognizes that, and *at the exact moment the dog's buttocks hits the ground the trainer clicks and offers the dog a reward.* Usually the reward is a small kernel sized food treat, but a reward can be a toy, play, or affection. Whatever the dog enjoys is a reward worth giving.

In as soon as 2-3 clicks have been issued a dog will associate the sound of the click with something it enjoys. Once the association is made, it will repeat the action it did when hearing the click. Click = Reward. When this goes off in the dog's head, repeating the action makes sense.

The three steps are as follows:

**1.** *Get the action* you request

**2.** *Mark the action* with your clicker

**3.** *Reinforce the action* with a reward

**How do you ask for actions when clicker training your dog?**

During clicker training before adding a cue command such as "stay," you wait until your dog completely understands the action. A cue is the name of the action or it can be a hand signal that you are using when you ask your dog to perform a specific action. Your dog should know the action *stay* from the click and reward before you verbally name it. *He or she has connected being still to receiving a click and reward.*

When training you do not want to add the *cue* until your dog has been clicked 5-10 times for the action, and is accurately responding in a manner that clearly shows he understands which action earns the click and reward. This is called introducing the cue.

Teaching your dog the name of the cue or action requires saying or signaling before your dog repeats the action. After several repetitions, begin to click and reward when your dog performs the action, be sure the cue is given before the reward. Your dog will learn to listen and watch for the cue, knowing that if he does the action a reward will follow.

**Clicker Training Help**

If your dog is not obeying the cue, answer the following questions and then revise your training process so that your dog knows the meaning of the clicker sound cue during all situations. Importantly, be sure that your dog is and feels rewarded for doing the correct action.

Trainers never assume the dog is intentionally disobeying without asking the questions below.

1. Does your dog understand the meaning of the cue?

2. Does your dog understand the meaning of the cue in the situation first taught, but *not* in the different situations that you gave the cue?

3. Is the *reward* for doing the action you want, satisfying your dog's needs? Is the treat or toy worth the effort?

Once you have answered these questions, change your training process to be certain that your dog understands the clicker/cue in all situations, including high distraction situations such as at a busy park. Then be sure your dog is adequately rewarded and that it is clear your dog feels that he or she has been properly rewarded. This will help put you two back on the path of mutual understanding during your training sessions.

## ~ *Paws On – Paws Off* ~

# 7 Let's Talk Treats

You are training your puppy and it is going well because your pup is the best dog in the world. *Oh yes he is, everyone knows this to be true.* Because of this fact, you want to make sure that you are giving your dog the right type of treats. Treats are easy, as long as you stay away from the things that aren't good for dogs, such as; avocados, onions, garlic, coffee, tea, caffeinated drinks, grapes, raisins, macadamia nuts, peaches, plums, pits, seeds, persimmons and chocolates.

Dog owners can make treats from many different foods. Treats should always be sized about the dimension of a kernel of corn. This makes them easy to grab from treat pouches and still flavorful enough for your hound to desire them.

All a dog needs is a little taste to keep them interested. The *kernel size* is something that is swiftly eaten and swallowed, thus not distracting from the training session. A treat is only to provide a quick taste, used for enticement and reinforcement, not as snack or meal.

When you are outdoors and there are many distractions, treats should be of a higher quality that is coveted by your pooch. Trainers call it a higher value treat because it is worthy of your dog breaking away from the activity they are engaged. Perhaps cubes of cheesed or dried and cooked meats will qualify as your dog's high value treat.

Make sure you mix up the types of treats by keeping a variety of treats available. Nothing is worse during training than when your puppy turns his nose up at a treat because he has grown bored of it or holds it to be of lesser value than his interests hold.

**Types of Treats**

Human foods that are safe for dogs include most fruits and veggies, cut up meats that are raw or cooked, yogurt, peanut butter, kibble, and whatever else you discover that your dogs like. Be sure that it is good for them, in particular their digestive system. Be advised that not all human foods are good for dogs. Please read about human foods that are acceptable for dogs and observe your dog's stools when introducing new treat ideas.

How many times have you heard a friend or family member tell you about some crazy food that their dog loves? Dogs do love a massive variety of foods; unfortunately, not all of the foods that they think they want to eat are good for them. Dog treating is not rocket science but it does take a little research, common sense and paying attention to how your dog reacts after wolfing down a treat.

Many people like to make homemade treats and that is okay, just keep to the rules we just mentioned and watch what you are adding while having fun in the kitchen. Remember to research and read the list of vegetables dogs can and cannot eat, and understand that pits and seeds can cause choking and intestinal issues such as dreaded doggy flatulence. When preparing, first remove any seeds and pits, and clean all fruits and veggies before slicing them into doggie size treats.

Before purchasing treats, look at the ingredients on the treat packaging and be sure there are no chemicals, fillers, additives, colors and things that are unhealthy. Some human foods that are tasty to us might not be so tasty to your dog and he will let you know. Almost all dogs love some type of raw or cooked meats. In tiny nibble sizes, these treats work great at directing their attention where you want it focused.

**Here are some treat ideas:**

- Whole grain cereals are good, such as cheerios without sugar added are a good choice.

- Kibble (dry foods). Put some in a paper bag and boost the aroma factor by tossing in some bacon or another meat product. Dogs are all about those yummy smell sensations.

- Beef Jerky that has no pepper or heavy seasoning added.

- Carrots, apple pieces, and some dogs even enjoy melons.

- Meats that have been cubed and are not highly processed or salted, these are easy to make at home as well. You can use cooked left over foods.

- Shredded cheese, string cheese or cubed cheese. Dogs love cheese!

- Cream cheese, peanut butter, or spray cheese. Give your dog a small dollop to lick for every proper behavior. These work well when training puppies to ring a bell to go outside for elimination.

- Baby food meat products, they certainly don't look yummy to us, but dogs adore them.

- Ice Cubes, but if your dog has dental problems, proceed cautiously.

- Commercial dog treats, but use caution, there are loads of them on the market. Look for those that do not have preservatives, by products, or artificial colors. Additionally, take into consideration the country of origin.

Never feed or treat your four-legged friend from the dining table, because you do not want to teach that begging actions are acceptable. When treating, give treats far from the dinner table or from areas that people normally gather to eat such as by the BBQ.

**Time to Treat**

The best time to issue dog treats is between meals. Treating too close to meal times makes all treats less effective, so remember this when planning your training sessions. If during training you need to refocus your dog back into the training session, keep a high value treat in reserve.

Obviously, if your dog is full from mealtime he will be less likely to want a treat reward than if a bit hungry. If your dog is not hungry, your training sessions will likely be more difficult and far less effective. This is why it is a good idea to reward correct actions with praise, play, or toys, and not to rely exclusively on treats.

- Love and attention are considered rewards and is certainly positive reinforcement that can be just as effective as an edible treat. Dog treating is comprised of edibles, praise, and attention. Engaging in play or allowing some quality time with their favorite rope toy is also effective and at times, these rewards are crucial to dog training.

- Do not give your dog a treat without asking for an action first. Say, "sit" and after your dog complies deliver the treat. This reinforces your training and their obedience.

- Avoid treating your dog when he is over stimulated and running amuck in an unfocused state of mind. This can be counterproductive and might *reinforce a negative behavior* resulting in the inability to get your dog's attention.

- Due to their keen sense of smell, they will know long before you could ever know that there is a tasty snack nearby, but keep it out of sight. Issue your command and wait for your dog to obey before presenting the reward. Remember when dog treating, it is important to be patient and loving, but it is equally important not to give the treat until your dog obeys.

- Some dogs have a natural gentleness to them and always take from your hand gently, while other dogs need some guidance to achieve this. If your dog is a bit rough during treat grabbing, go ahead and train the command "gentle!" when giving treats. Be firm from this point forward. Give no treats unless they are gently taken from your hand. Remain steadfast with your decision to implement this, and soon your pup will comply if he wants the tasty treat.

## Bribery vs. Reward Dog Treating

The other day a friend of mine mentioned *bribing* for an action that he had commanded. I thought about it later and thought I would clarify for my readers. *Bribery* is the act of offering the food visually in advance so that the dog will act out a command or alter a behavior. *Reward* is giving your dog his favorite toy, treat, love, or affection *after* he has performed the commanded action.

An example of bribery would happen when you want your dog to come, and *before* you call your dog, you hold a cube of steak for them to see. Reward would be giving your dog the steak after they have obeyed the *come* command. Never show the treats before issuing commands.

Bribed dogs learn to comply with your wishes *only when they see food*. The rewarded dog realizes that they only receive rewards after performing the desired actions. This also assists by introducing non-food items as rewards when training and treating.

## ~ *Paws On – Paws Off* ~

# Health Insurance
## for my Dog?
### *Really?* Why?

**Because Paying Cash Makes No "Cents" or Does It?**

*Shocking Statistics!* **Discover the Truth!**

**Type Into Your Browser**

**nobrainerdogtrainer.com/insurance-for-dogs/**

# PART II BEGIN SCHOOL

# 8 Housetraining the Westie

When you first bring your pee and poop machine home, clip on his leash and carry him to the predetermined waste elimination spot that you and your family have chosen. Let your pup eliminate his waste and then take him inside. Now that you have established his elimination spot remind the family that is where your pup should be taken each time he has to eliminate.

Next, bring him inside and place him inside his pen. This is particularly important if you have other pets and dogs inside your house. The pen acts as a barrier so that the first interactions are not frightening or god forbid, harmful. This allows the pup gradually to become accustomed to your other pets and humans inside the house.

The pen should already have been set up in the chosen spot where he can be close to the family. If on carpet then a tarp should be laid down and then covered with newspaper and pee pads. Inside should be chew-toys, crate, water bowl, and a soft bed or blanket for him to rest and sleep. This will be your pup's new home for much of the first months while being housetrained and crate-trained.

Do not over handle your puppy during the first hour's home, because he needs to adjust to the new surroundings and all the creatures inside, let him approach using his own will. Additionally, when you do take him out of his pen to begin gradual socialization and let him explore, your house should be completely puppy-proofed to avoid injury to him. This should have been done prior to you bringing your puppy home, but it's a good idea to perform a second check for exposed electrical cords and anything he might be able to put into his mouth and cause him to choke or do self-harm.

It is a fact that dogs are a bit particular about where they "relieve" themselves and will invariably build a strong habit. While housetraining your puppy, remember that whenever he *soils somewhere* in the house, he is building a strong preference to that particular area. This is why preventing soiling accidents is very important; additionally thoroughly cleaning the area where the defecation or urination has occurred is tremendously important. When your puppy does relieve his self in the house, *blame yourself* not your pup.

Until your puppy has learned where he is supposed to do his business, you should keep a constant, watchful eye on him, whether he is in his crate, on a mat, beside you or in his pen. During housetraining, some people will *tether* their puppies to their waist or to a nearby object. This allows them to keep their puppies in eyesight at all times.

- When your pup is indoors but out of the crate, watch for sniffing or circling, and as soon as you see this behavior, take him outdoors right away. *Do not hesitate.*

- If your pup is having accidents in the crate, the crate may be too big. The crate should be big enough for your puppy to stand up, turn around, and lie down in. If crate accidents occur, remove any soiled items from the crate and thoroughly clean it.

- Keep your puppy confined to their specific gated puppy area where accidents can be easily cleaned, such as his pen or section of bathroom, pantry, laundry, or similar. Do not leave your puppy confined to their crate for hours upon end. You want their crate to be an enjoyable place that they find safe and comforting.

- Set a timer to go off every forty-five minutes to an hour so that you remember to take your puppy out before nature calls. With progress, you can increase the time duration between elimination outings.

- A good rule of thumb for elimination outing frequencies is as follows

• Up to six weeks of age, elimination every 45 minutes - hour.

• Two months of age, around two to three hours.

• Three months, four hours.

- Four months and up - around five hours.

These times will vary a little with individual dogs.

- If your pup doesn't do his *duty* when taken outdoors, after a few minutes bring him back indoors and keep a close eye on him. One option is to keep your pup tethered to your waist so that he is always in eyesight, then try again in 10-15 minutes.

- While you are away, if possible, arrange to have a person to take your puppy outside to eliminate because this will greatly speed up the housetraining process.

## Establish a Schedule

- You should take your puppy out many times during the day, most importantly after eating, playing, or sleeping. Feed your puppy appropriate amounts of food three times per day and leave the food down for around fifteen-minutes at a time, then remove it. You can keep a pups water down until about eight at night, but then remove it from your puppy's reach. This will help with accidents and waking up less in the night to bear the elements while he does his business.

- When you hear him whining, take him out for elimination once during the night. Puppies can usually hold their bladders for about 4-5 hours during sleep. Dogs do not like to soil their own area and only as a last resort will they soil their crate or bedding.

- Gradually, your puppy will be able to hold his urine for increasingly longer lengths of time, but until then keep to the every hour schedule unless he is sleeping, but always take him out after waking. Having your puppy's excrement and urine outdoors will put your puppy's housetraining on the fast track.

## Consistency Is the Mother of Prevention

Until your puppy is reliably housetrained, bring him outside to the same spot each time, and always leaving a little bit of his waste there as a scent marker. This will be the designated relief spot, and if you like can place a warning sign at that spot. Remember to use this spot for *relief* only and not for play. Bring your puppy to his spot, and when you see him getting ready to eliminate waste, say something like "potty time," "hurry up," or "now."

As your pup is eliminating, do not speak, because it will distract him and potentially interrupt full elimination. Instead, ponder how much fun it will be when he is playing fetch and running back to you. When your puppy finishes, praise, pet, give a top-notch treat, and spend about five minutes playing with him. If he does not relieve himself, take your pup inside, keep an eye on him, and try again in 10-15 minutes.

If your puppy eliminates in the house, remember, that it is *your fault*. Maybe you went too quickly. If you see your puppy relieving himself in the wrong spot, quickly bring him outside to the designated potty spot so that he can finish there, then when he is done, offer praise for finishing in the correct spot.

If you find a mess, clean it thoroughly without your puppy watching you do it. Use a cleaner made specifically for pet stains so that there is no smell or evidence that you have failed him. This way it will not become a regular spot for your puppy and a new regular clean up chore for you. Regular outings should keep this chore to a minimum.

**This Question Rings a Bell: Can I teach my puppy when to tell me when he needs to go out?**

- Yes, you can! Hang a bell at dog level beside the door you use to let your pup outdoors. Put a dab of easy cheese or peanut butter on the bell. When he touches the bell and it rings, immediately open the door. Repeat this every time and take him to the potty spot. Eventually, he will ring the bell without the food on it and this will tell you when he needs to go outside.

Be careful here, your puppy may start to ring the bell when he wants to go outside to play, explore, or other non-elimination reasons. To avoid this, each time he rings the bell, *only* take him out to the potty spot. If he starts to play, immediately bring him in the house reinforcing that the bell means elimination only.

Now that the schedule has been established and you know what you are supposed to do, keep in mind that puppies can generally hold for a good one-hour stretch. Adult larger breeds of dogs can hold their bladders longer than smaller dog breeds and some small dogs cannot last the night before needing to go outside. Most adult dogs generally do not last longer than 8-10 hours between needing to urinate.

*Housetraining* completion ranges from six months to twelve months. A dogs personality contributes to the training length of time. By four months most puppies often know to wait, but might still have issues. Many puppies are housetrained by six to eight months, or mostly trained by six months with occasional accidents lasting a further few months.

All dog owners are much happier after this training is completed but keep in mind that scolding your dog for doing a natural thing *is not going to help you* in housetraining. Rewarding him for the outdoor eliminations and *avoiding* indoor accidents is your gateway to success.

Of course, when you see your pup about to pee or poop indoors, a quick "No" as you sweep him up to take him outside might temporarily cease the activity so that you can whisk them outside before any waste hits the ground or possibly your hand and arm. Then as previously mentioned, praise at the beginning of the outdoor elimination then remain quiet.

It isn't as difficult as it might seem. Being active in housetraining will definitely speed up the process, but it does take a few months for puppies to increase their bladder abilities and to learn. Too often new puppy owners are not around enough to follow the protocol efficiently and this regularly leads to housetraining taking longer. Some dogs learn suprisingly fast that outdoors is the only acceptable place to eliminate waste, but their bodies haven't matured to catch up to their brain function, so please practice patience and understanding.

## *~ Paws On – Paws Off ~*

# 9 Crate Training

Dogs need their own safe place to call home and relax. An owner's house might be a place to roam, but it's not the den that dogs crave. The crate satisfies a dog's longing for a den, and along with its many other uses provides comfort to them. All puppies should be taught to enjoy residing in their crate and know that it is a safe haven for them, so it is important *never* to use it for punishment.

Before you begin crate training give your dog a couple of days to adjust to his new home and surroundings. Crate training can be trained for a dog of any age. A dog's love for their crate is healthy and assists you in taking care of him or her throughout their lifetime.

Try to limit your puppy's time in the crate to around one hour per session. Never leave your adult dog in a crate for longer than five hours without providing them time outside of the crate. As your puppy matures and has learned proper dog etiquette (not chewing everything in sight), is housetrained, and can be trusted to run freely around your house, you can then leave the door open so that they can use it for their private bungalow to come and go as they choose.

I have listed below the benefits of crate, things to avoid, types, furnishings, the steps to crate train your dog, and troubleshooting, Godspeed.

**Benefits of the Crate**

- It aids in housetraining because dogs are reluctant to soil their own sleeping area.

- Acts as a mobile doghouse for trips via car, airplane, train and then to be used at destinations such as motels, and foreign houses.

- The mobility can be utilized inside your own home by being moved throughout the house. *Especially beneficial during housetraining when you want your puppy near you.

- Can reduce separation anxiety.

- Keep your dog out of harm's way.

- Assists in chew-toy addiction.

- Aids your puppy in calming and quieting down.

Until he or she has learned that chewing, tearing, ripping of household and human items is forbidden, the crate keeps your dog shortly separated from destruction of those items.

**Things to Avoid**

- *Do not use the crate as punishment*. If used in this manner it will defeat the purpose and cause your dog to fear the crate instead of love it.

- *Avoid lengthy crating sessions*. Long periods in the crate defer socialization, exercise, and lend to doggy depression, anxiousness, and anxiety.

- Puppies have an issue holding their need to eliminate waste. Young puppies tend to go hourly, but as they mature, the time between elimination lengthens. Keep this in mind for puppies and adult dogs, and always schedule elimination breaks. Set a timer to remind you to let your dog outdoors.

A good rule of thumb for elimination intervals is as follows, up to six weeks of age - elimination every hour, at two months of age - around two to three hours, at three months - four hours, four months and up - around five hours. These times will vary with individual dogs.

If you are housetraining an adult dog, he or she might be able to hold their bowels longer, but have not yet learned that they are required to wait and go outdoors.

- *Soiled items*. Quickly remove and clean any soiled items inside the crate, and thoroughly clean the crate with a non-toxic cleaner that will erase any signs of elimination. Dogs are creatures of habit and will think it is okay to eliminate where they have previously eliminated.

- Avoid crating your dog when your dog has not recently eliminated waste.

- Avoid continued involuntary crating after your puppy is housetrained and he or she understands that damaging human property is forbidden; instead only use the crate when necessary.

## Buying, Furnishing, and Preparing the Crate

The time has come for you to go crate shopping and you notice that they come in many sizes and design options. Let the shopper in you compare the advantages and disadvantages of the different styles to figure out which will be best suited for your usage and dog. A few types are as follows, collapsible metal, metal with fabric, wire, solid plastic, fixed and folding aluminum, and soft-sided collapsible crates that conveniently fold up easily for travel.

Regarding traveling be sure always to have your dog safely secured when in a motor vehicle. There are crates specially designed and tested for vehicle transportation.

### "What size crate do I purchase?"

The crate should be big enough for your puppy to stand up, turn around, and lie down in. If you wish to hedge your bet, instead of purchasing multiple crates you can purchase a crate that will accommodate your puppy when full size, but this will require blocking off the end so that they are unable to eliminate waste in a section and then move to another that is apart from where they soiled.

In summary, per the criteria mentioned above, you need to cordon off the crate to accommodate your puppy's smaller size and then expand as he or she grows.

### "What do I put into the crate?"

Toys, treats, blanket or mat and the entire home furnishings a young puppy needs and desires to be entertained. Avoid televisions, tablets, and radios. Seriously, you should provide an ample supply of natural material indestructible chew-toys, and things such as indestructible balls. All of the chews and toys should be large enough not to be swallowed, and tough enough to withstand tearing apart a portion that could be swallowed by your puppy. Treats will be occasionally required, and stuffing them into the chew-toys will occupy the young pup for hours.

Clean water is another essential item that all dogs must have regular access. You can utilize a small rodent type water dispenser attached to the side of the crate. If you know that your dog will only be in the crate under two hours, then he or she will probably be able to go without water.

*"Where do I place the crate?"*

It is a good idea to place the crate close to where you are located in the house. This keeps a puppy from feeling lonely and you able to keep an eye out for signs that he or she needs to eliminate waste. As housetraining is successful, the crate does not have to be located beside you, only near you, or in central location to where you are working or relaxing. Eventually the crate can be located at further distances, but you do not want your dog ever to feel isolated.

# Introducing Your Dog to the Crate

These steps will help your dog to adjust to his crate and associate it with good things such as security, comfort, and a quiet place to ponder the meaning of life, things such as why he or she walks on four legs and humans on two, and how does my food magically appear.

Never force your dog into the crate by using physical means of persuasion. Crate training should be a natural process that takes place on your dog's time schedule. Curious dogs might immediately begin to explore the inner domain while others take some time, and possibly some coaxing by using lures such as toys and food. Let the process proceed in small steps and gradually your dog will want to spend more time in his new five-star luxury crate. This training can proceed very quickly or take days to complete.

**Phase I**

*1.* Set the crate in a common area and check that all of the crates goodies are inside, chew-toys, blanket or towel. Open and secure the door. If your dog does not mosey on over in his or her own accord, then place them near the crate entrance and give him a pep talk using your happy-go-lucky fun voice. Wait a bit and see if his curiosity kicks in and he begins to explore the inner domain.

2. If your pep talk and shining personality are not sparking his curiosity then go to plan B, food lures. To begin, you don't have to use anything fancy, just use his normal puppy food. Drop some in the back of the crate and a couple closer to the front door, and see if that gets his little tail wagging and paws moving. After you place the food inside step away and give him some room to make his own decisions. Do not force anything. Just observe throughout the day and see if your dog is venturing inside or near the crate. Do this a few times throughout the day.

...ork, try it again. If he is still disinterested, you can also ...w-toy into the crate and ask him to find his toy and see ...to the crate.

...g this process until your dog will walk all of the way into ...ieve the food or toy. This step is sometimes accomplished ... it can take a couple of days. Be sure to praise your dog for succe... ...ntering. Do not shut the door. Observe whether they are calm, timid, or frightened.

5. Once your dog is regularly entering his crate without fear, you can move onto phase II.

**Phase II**

Phase II will help if your dog is not acting as though his crate is a place that he wants to enter and remain, and might be showing signs of fear or anxiety when inside. This phase will help warm him up to his crate.

By using feeding time, you can reinforce that the crate is a place that your dog should enjoy. During Phase II training, remain in the presence of your dog's crate or at least in the same room. Later you will begin leaving the room where he is crated.

1. Start by feeding your dog in front of his crate door. Feeding your dog near his crate will create a nice association with the crate. *If your dog already enters his crate freely, set the food bowl inside that he has to enter the crate to eat.

2. Next, place his food bowl far enough into the crate that your dog has to step inside to eat. Then each following time that you feed him place the bowl further inside.

3. When your dog will stand and eat inside his crate, and you know that he is calm and relaxed, then you can close the crate door while he eats his meal.

The first time, immediately open the door when he finishes his meal. Then after each successive meal, leave the door closed for longer durations. For example, after meal completion, two, three, four minutes, and then incrementally increasing until you reach ten to fifteen minutes. Stay diligent and if you notice your dog begins frantically whining or is acting anxious, back up and then slow down on the time increases.

4. If your dog continues whining the next time, then leave him in there until he calms. *This is important*, because you cannot reinforce that whining is a way out of the crate, or a way always to get your attention or manipulate.

5. Now that he is comfortable entering, eating, and spending some time in his crate, move onto Phase III, which explains about training your dog to enjoy spending more time in the crate with you around and out of the house.

## Phase III

This is where you will continue increasing the time duration that your dog is crated. First, be certain that he is not displaying signs of fear or anxiety. Whining and whimpering does not always signify that anxiety is present. It is often a tool used when they want some attention from their mom or humans. It is a sympathy tool honed sharp when they were weening on mothers milk.

If you choose at this point, you can begin issuing a command that goes with your crating action. For example, say "crate," "home," "cage," "cave," or whatever is simple and natural. Maybe cage sounds negative to us, but your dog does not know the difference.

1. Stand next to the crate with his favorite toy and then call him over to you and give the command "cave," while placing the toy inside. A hand signal that you choose can also be used along with this command, but make sure that you do not use the same hand signal for another command. As an option, you can use a favored treat instead of a toy.

When he enters, praise him, shut the door, and let him stay inside for duration of ten to fifteen minutes. You should remain close to the crate. Do this a few times separated by an hour or two. During dog training, gradually proceeding is always a good rule to follow.

2. Repeat the step above, but this time only stay nearby for about five minutes, and then leave the room for an additional ten to fifteen minutes. When you return, do not rush over to the crate, instead remain in the room for a few more minutes and then let your dog out of the crate. It is not necessary to physically remove him, just open the door.

Repeat this five to seven times per day and gradually increase the duration that your dog remains in the crate. Work your way up to 30-40 minutes when you are completely out of sight. *Do not forget to use your vocal command and physical cue every time that you want your dog to enter his crate.*

3. Continue increasing the time that he is crated while you are home. Work up to one hour.

4. Next, place the crate near your room and let him sleep the night inside the crate near where you are sleeping such as in the doorway or just

outside your bedroom. At this time, you can also begin to leave your dog crated when you need to leave the house for short durations of under two hours.

A good way to begin is to leave your dog in his crate while you are outdoors doing yard work. Remember that when your return inside, to act casual and normal. Do what you need upon returning inside, and then open the crate door and then secure the opened door.

*Puppies usually need to eliminate waste during the night, thus you will need to make some late night trips outdoors.

As your dog becomes accustomed to his crate and surroundings, you can begin gradually to move the crate to your preferred location, but not to an isolated place.

## Tips & Troubleshooting

● In the beginning, especially with puppies, keep the crate close to where you are in the house, and sleeping at night. As mentioned, you want to avoid any negative associations such as isolation that can result in depression or contribute to separation anxiety. This also strengthens your bond, and allows easy access for late night elimination trips.

Due to bladder and bowel control, puppies under six months should be kept crated for periods *under* four hours.

● Ignore whining unless your dog responds to your elimination command or phrase that you have been using when taking him to his elimination spot. If he does respond, then you know that he was whining for that and not simply for attention.

I know it is difficult to ignore whining, but it must be done so that your new dog or puppy understands that you are not at their disposal every time they seek attention. If you are bonding, socializing and practicing the other items suggested, then your puppy or dog should not need the extra attention.

● Before crating, take your dog outdoors to eliminate. There should be only 5-15 minutes between elimination and crating. *Best chance for success for your dog not to soil his crate.

● Don't forget to leave plenty of fresh water, chew-toys, and items that require problem solving, such as food stuffed toys.

● Don't place your dog into the crate for long periods before your departure from the house. Try to keep it under fifteen minutes or less.

Fluctuate the time between crating and departure.

- When soiling accidents occur inside the crate, thoroughly clean the crate and its contents with a *pet odor neutralizer*. Warning, do not use ammonia.

- *A couple of warnings* regarding crating - Avoid crating in direct sunlight or excessive heat, if your dog is sick with diarrhea or vomiting, or is having bowel and urine control issues. You can resume training once these are resolved.

- Always provide sufficient exercise and socialization.

- Never use the crate as a form of punishment.

- Quick review of approximate crating times per age, are as follows, 9-10 weeks 30-60 minutes, 11-14 weeks 1-3 hrs., 15-16 weeks 3-4 hrs., 17 + weeks 4-6 hrs.

- To thwart separation anxiety issues, never make a big emotional showing when you leave the house. Always act normal, because it is a normal thing for you to come and go. Do the same when you return, do not over dramatize your return, first do what you need to do then casually go over to his crate and open the door without making a big show of it. This aids your dog in understanding that all of this coming and going is a *normal* part of his life.

- After your dog is housetrained, and is no longer destructive, do not forcibly crate your dog, except when you absolutely need them crated. During other times, leave the door securely open and allow them to voluntarily come and go as they choose.

- Some reasons that your dog continues to soil his own crate are as follows. The crate is too large; there is a diet issue, health issue, too young to have control, suffering severe separation anxiety, or has drunk too much water prior to crating.

Another contributing factor could be the manner that your dog was housed prior to your acquiring him. If he was confined continuously to a small enclosure with no other outlet for elimination this will cause issues with housetraining and crating. If this is true for your dog, training will require more time and patience.

- Separation anxiety is an issue that cannot be solved using a crate. Consult the diagnosing and solving separation anxiety guidelines.

That wraps up crate training. I wish you well in crate and housetraining. I am sure that you will do wonderfully in shaping your dog's behaviors.

# 10 Clicker Response Training

**Important** - *Conceal the treat!* <u>*Do not* show your puppy the treat before depressing the clicker button,</u> and never deliver the treat prior to the clicker emitting a clicking sound. If you do this, your puppy will be responding to the treat and not the click, and this will undermine your training strategy.

Training should begin by simply observing your Westie puppy. What you are looking for is a desired behavior to reward. In other words, if your puppy is doing anything considered as an undesirable behavior, then do not reward. As long as your puppy is relaxed and behaving well, you can begin to train using this clicker response training. What you are doing here is training your puppy to associate the clicker sound with doing something good. Whenever you click, your puppy will associate the sound with an acceptable performance, and will know that he or she has a reward coming.

Timing is crucial when training your puppy. The essential technique when training your puppy with the clicker is by clicking precisely as the correct action takes place, followed by treating. It does not take long for your puppy to associate their behavior with the clicking sound, and subsequent receiving of a treat. Make sure that the treat is produced *immediately* following the clicking sound.

Note: Throughout this training guide, *Click and Treat is sometimes written as C/T.* In addition, for ease of writing, I refer to the gender of your dog in the male form, even though I know many people have female dogs. Please take no offense to this.

**Crucial** – *Never click without treating, and never treat without clicking. This maintains the connection and continuity between clicking and treating, which is the framework for achieving your desired outcomes.*

**Steps**

**1.** When your puppy is relaxed, you should stand, or kneel down at about an arm's length away, then click and give your puppy a treat.

**2.** Repeat this clicking and treating about 5-15 times. Pause a few seconds between clicks to allow your puppy to resume whatever he was doing. Do not click and treat if he seems to be begging for another treat. Find times throughout the day when he is performing a desired behavior, then click and treat. This teaches your puppy to associate the click with what you want him to do, and a tasty food treat.

When you click, and your puppy's head swings around in anticipation of a treat, then you know that your puppy has made the association between the clicking sound and a reward.

**4.** Repeat steps one and two the day following the introduction of clicker training. When your puppy quickly responds to the click, then you can begin using the clicker to train commands.

Teaching puppies to respond to this method can take several training sessions, but most commonly after about a dozen click and treats, they begin to connect the clicking sound with a treat. Usually, at the end of the first 5-minute session, puppies tend to swing their head around when they hear the clicker sound.

**HELPFUL HINT:** After some dedicated training sessions, puppies tend to stop in their tracks and instantly come to you for a treat. At this time refrain from using this clicker technique to get your dog to *come* to you, but instead follow the instructions for teaching the "come" command.

# 11  Name Recognition

After your puppy responds to the clicking sound, and he knows very well that treats follow the clicking sound, you can now begin teaching him commands and tricks. Now, we are going to teach your puppy some specific things. Let's start with the base exercise that is teaching your puppy to respond to his or her *name*. I assume that you have already gone through the painstaking process of naming your puppy, and now when his or her name is spoken you want your puppy to learn to respond. This can be easy, fun, and satisfying when you finally get positive results.

Teaching your puppy his name is a basic and necessary objective that must be accomplished in order to gain and keep your puppies attention during further training.

Before beginning training, be sure to gather an ample variety of treats. Put these treats in your pockets, treat pouch, or on a tabletop out of sight, and out of your puppy's reach.

**1.** Ignore your puppy until he looks directly at you, when he does, *click and treat* him. Repeat this 10-15 times. This teaches your puppy to associate the click with a treat, when he looks in your direction.

**2.** Next, when your puppy looks at you, begin adding your puppy's name, spoken right before you *click and treat.*

**3.** Continue doing this until your puppy will look at you when you say his or her name.

**4.** Gradually phase out clicking and treating your puppy every time that he or she looks at you. Decrease C/T incrementally; one out of two times, then one out of three, four, and then not at all. Try not to phase out the C/T too quickly.

After successful name recognition training, you should C/T on occasion, to refresh your puppy's memory and reinforce the association to hearing his name, and receiving a treat. Observe your puppy's abilities and pace during this training process, and adjust appropriately, when needed. The ultimate goal is to have your puppy obey all the commands via vocal or physical cue, *without a reward.*

Responding to his or her name is the most important learned behavior, because it is the base skill of all future training. Therefore, you will want to give this training a considerable amount of attention, and thoroughly complete before moving on.

I advise that you repeat this exercise in various locations around your home, while he is out on the leash, outside in the yard, or in the park. Eventually, make sure that you practice this while there are distractions, such as when there are guests present, when his favorite toys are visible, when there is food around, and when he is among other dogs. Always maintain *good eye contact* when you are calling your puppy's name. Keep on practicing this name recognition exercise until there is no doubt that when you speak your puppy's name, he or she knows whom you are referring to, and they respond appropriately.

It may sound odd, but also try the training when you are in different physical positions, such as sitting, standing, kneeling or lying down. Mix it up so that he gets used to hearing his name in a variety of areas and situations, and repeat this process frequently. No matter the situation, this command *must* be obeyed.

Name recognition will avoid trouble later on down the line. For example, if your puppy gets into something that he should not, such as a scrap with another dog, chasing a cat or squirrel, or far worse, getting involved in a time-share pyramid scheme, you can simply call your puppy's name to gain his attention and then redirect him. You invariably want your puppy to come no matter what the distraction, so training "come" is also a crucial command to teach, and regularly practice throughout the lifetime of your dog. Remember, your puppy first needs to know his or her name so that you can teach these other commands.

To be certain that you are able to grab your dog's attention in any circumstance or situation, continue to practice this training into adulthood to reinforce the behavior. When your puppy is appropriately responding to his or her name, I recommend moving forward to the "come" command.

### ~ *Paws On – Paws Off* ~

# 12 "Come"

After your puppy recognizes, and begins responding to his name being called, then the "come" command takes priority as the first command to teach. *Why?* Because this one could save his life, save your sanity, and avoid you the embarrassment of running through the neighborhood in the middle of the night wearing little more than a robe and slippers, pleading for your dog to return.

If by chance, he is checking out the olfactory magic of the trash bin, the best way to redirect your dog is firmly command him to *"come,"* followed immediately by a reward when he complies. Petting, verbal praise, or play is an appropriate reinforcement and an effective redirecting incentive during this type of situation.

In order to grab your dog's attention, no matter what activity he is engaged in, it is necessary to implement an effective verbal command. Unfortunately, the word *"come"* is a commonly used word that is spoken regularly during daily life, thus making it difficult to isolate as a special command word, so I suggest that a unique and infrequently used word be chosen for this. With my dog Axel, I use "jax" as my replacement word for *come*. For example, I say "Axel *jax*," which replaces the standard, "Axel *come*," or "Axel *here.*" When your dog hears this special cue word, he will recognize it as the word associated with the command to return to you and receive a special treat. However, there is nothing wrong with simply using "come" as your command word if you find it effective and natural.

*Note:* Choose a command word with one or two syllables, and one that you can easily say, because it will be difficult to change the substituted "come" command word later.

**Here's what to do-**

- If you have chosen to use a unique "come" command, you can begin here. We will not use the clicker at this time. First, gather your assortment of treats such as bits of steak, bacon, or whatever your dog most covets.

Begin with the tastiest treat in hand, and speak the new command word, immediately followed by a treat. When your dog hears this new word, he will begin to associate it with a special treat. Keep repeating this exercise, and mix up the treats that you provide. Remember to conclude each training session by providing a lot of praise to your dog. Repeat for about ten repetitions then proceed onto the next step.

- Gather your clicker and treats, and then find a quiet, low distraction place so that both of you can focus. First, place a treat on the floor and walk to the other side of the room. Next, hold out a hand with a visible treat in it. Now, say your dog's name to get his attention, followed by the command "come." Use a pleasant, happy tone when you do this.

When your dog begins to move towards you, press the clicker, and praise him all the way to the treat in your hand. The objective of this is for him to ignore the treat on the ground and come to you. When he gets to you, *treat* him from your hand and offer some more praise and affection. Be sure and not click again, only give the treat.

Each time your dog comes to you, pet or touch his head and grab a hold of his collar before treating. Sometimes do this on top of the collar, and sometimes beneath his head on the bottom of the collar. This action gets your dog used to being held, so when you need to grab a hold of him by the collar he will not shy away or fight you.

Do this 10-12 times, and then take a break. Make sure that your dog accomplishes the task by walking the complete distance across the room to you, while wholly ignoring the treat that you placed on the floor.

- For the next session, you will need the assistance of a family member. First, situate yourselves at a distance of about 5-6 paces opposite each other, and place a treat on the floor between the two of you. Each of you show your dog a treat when you say his name followed by "come." Now, take turns calling your dog back and forth between the two of you. Treat and praise your dog each time he successfully comes all of the way to either of you, *while ignoring the treat*. Repeat this about a dozen times. The objective of this exercise is to reinforce the idea that coming when commanded is not only for you, but is beneficial to him as well.

- This time, grab your clicker. As before, put a treat on the ground, move across the room, and then call your dog's name to get his attention, but this time hold out an empty hand and give the command. This will mess with him a little, but that's okay, he's learning. As soon as he starts to come to you, give him praise and when he reaches you, *click and treat* by using the opposite hand that you were luring him. If your dog is not completing the distance to you, press the clicker as he begins to move closer to you, and the first time he completes the distance, give him a supersized treat serving (7-10 treats). Each additional time your dog comes all of the way to you; reward your dog with a regular sized treat serving. Do this about a dozen times, and then take a break.

- Keep practicing this exercise, but now call your dog using an empty hand. Using this technique over several sessions and days should eventually result in a successful hand signal command. Following your dog's consistent compliance with this hand signal training, you can then take the training to the next step by phasing out the hand signal by using only a verbal cue. When shifting to the verbal cue training, reduce treating incrementally, first by treating one out of two times, then one out three times, followed by one out of four, five, six, and lastly without treating at all.

Note: It is important to treat your dog periodically in order to reinforce the desired behavior that he is exhibiting, as well as complying with the command you are issuing. Make sure your dog is coming when commanded; this includes all family members and friends. By the end of this section, your dog should consistently be obeying the hand signal and the verbal "come" commands successfully.

**Let's get complex**

- Now, by adding distractions we will begin to make obeying commands a more difficult task for your dog. The outcome of this training should result in better control over your pooch in times when there is distracting stimulus.

First, find somewhere where there are sights, sounds, and even smells that might distract your dog. Just about anything can serve as a distraction, here. You can intentionally implement distractions, such as having his favorite toy in hand, by having another person present, or even doing this training beside the half of roast ox that is on the rotisserie in the back yard. Indoors, distractive aspects of daily home life, such as cooking, the noise of the television, the doorbell, or friends and family coming and going can serve as distractions. Even move to calling your dog from different rooms of the house, meanwhile gradually introducing other distractions such as music from the stereo, groups of people and combinations of the sort. Of course, the outdoor world is a megamall of potential interruptions, commotions and interferences for your pal to be tantalized and diverted by.

- *During this training exercise, I find it helpful to keep a log of not only how your dog is progressing, but also accounting for the different kinds and levels of distractions your dog is encountering.*

Now, in the high stimulus setting, resume training using the previous set of learned commands. As before, begin with treats in hand, because in this instance, when necessary, the snacks will act as a lure for your dog to follow in order to help him focus, rather than as a reward. The goal is to dispense with the treats by gradually phasing them out, eventually only using the vocal command.

When outdoors with your dog, practice calling the command "come" when you and your dog are in the yard with another animal or person, followed by increasing and more complex distractions. Such as a combination of a person and animal together, then with multiple people conversing or while children are running around, and then you can even throw some toys or balls into the mix.

Eventually, move out onto the streets and sidewalks, introducing even busier locations, remembering to keep track of your dog's progress as the situations become more and more distracting. The goal is that you want your dog to come every time you call "come," no matter how much noise and movement is happening around him.

If your dog consistently begins to return to you seven or eight times out of each ten commands, regardless of the distractions, this shows that the two of you are making very good progress, and that you are well on your way to the ideal goal of nine out of ten times compliant. If your dog is sporting ten out of ten times, you may consider enrolling him at an Ivy League university, or paying a visit to NASA, because you've got yourself one special canine there.

We all want a dog that comes when you use the "come" command. Whether he is seven houses down the road, or just in the next room, a dog that comes to you no matter what he is engaged in, is a dog worth spending the time training.

**Interrupting Fetch Exercises, Hide & Seek, and the Decoy Exercise**

Practice all of the following exercises with increasing distractions, both indoors and outdoors. Focus on practicing one of these exercises per session, eventually mixing up the order of the exercises as your dog masters each. Remember it is always important to train in a safe area.

*- Interrupting Fetch Exercises*

Get an ample-sized handful of your Westies favorite treat. Then, lob a ball or a piece of food at a reasonable distance, and as your dog is in the process of chasing it, call him by issuing the *come* command. If he comes *after* he gets the ball/food, give your dog a little reward of one piece of treat. If he comes *before* he gets the ball/food, give your dog a supersized (7-10) serving of treats.

If your dog is not responding to your "come" command, then throw the ball and quickly place a treat down towards his nose height while at the same time saying, "come", when he comes to you click and supersize treat your dog. Then, begin phasing out the treat lure.

After you have thrown the ball/food over several sessions, it is time to change it up. Like the exercise prior, this time you will fake throwing something, and then call your dog. If your dog goes looking for the ball/food before he comes back to you, give a small treat. If he comes immediately after you say, "come," give the supersized treat portion. Repeat this exercise 7-10 times.

*- Hide & Seek*

While you are both outside, and your dog is distracted and does not seem to know you exist, quickly *hide* from him. When your dog comes looking for you, and eventually finds you, *click and treat* your dog in addition with lots of love and praise. By adding a little drama, make it seem like an extremely big deal that your dog has found you. This is something that you can regularly practice and reward.

*- The Decoy*

One person calls the dog; we will call this person the *trainer*. One person tries to distract the dog with food and toys; we will call this person the *decoy*. After the trainer calls the dog, if the dog goes toward the decoy, the decoy person should turn away from the dog and neither of you offer rewards. When the dog goes towards the trainer, he should be rewarded by *both* the trainer and the decoy. Repeat 7-10 times.

**HELPFUL HINTS**

- Let your dog know that his coming to you is always the best thing ever, sometimes offering him supersized treat rewards for this behavior. Always reward by treating or praising, and when appropriate you can add play with a favorite toy or ball.

- Never, call your Westie for something he might find unpleasant. To avoid this disguise the real purpose. If you are leaving the field where he has been running, call your dog, put on the leash, and play a little more before leaving. If you are calling your dog to get him into the bath, provide a few minutes of affection or play instead of leading him straight into the bath. This will pacify and distract from any negative association with coming to you.

- You are calling, and your puppy is not responding. What do you do now? Try running backwards away from your dog, crouch, and clap, or show your dog a toy or food. When he comes, still reward him even if he has stressed you out. Running *towards* your dog signals to play *catch me*, so avoid doing this.

- If your dog has been enjoying some unabated freedom off lead, remember to give him a C/T when he checks in with you. Later you can phase out the C/T and only use praise.

- You should practice "come" five to ten times daily, ongoing for life. This command is one of those potentially life-saving commands that helps with all daily activities and interactions. The goal is that your dog will come running to you, whether you are in or out of sight, and from any audible distance. As owners, we know that having a dog that obeys this command makes dog things less stressful.

## ~ *Paws On – Paws Off* ~

# 13 "Drop it"

Teaching your Westie to *drop-it* is very important. *Why?* Well, if you have ever had a young puppy, you know that it is one giant mouth gobbling up whatever is in sight. Rumor has it that Stephen Hawking actually got the idea of the black hole from his puppy's ever-consuming mouth. Joking aside, sometimes valuable and dangerous things go into that mouth, and the command to "drop it" may save your family heirloom, over even perhaps your dog's life.

If you teach your dog correctly, when you give the command "drop it," he will open his mouth and drop whatever is in there. Most importantly, he will not only drop the item, but he will allow you to retrieve it without protest. When teaching the *drop-it* command you must offer a good trade for what your dog has in his mouth. You need to *out-treat* your dog by offering a better treat of higher value in exchange for what he has in his mouth. In addition, it is a good idea to stay calm and not to chase your puppy, as this elicits a play behavior that can work against your desired training outcomes.

If this command is successfully taught, your puppy will actually enjoy hearing "drop it." This command will also build trust between the two of you. In example, if you say, "drop it," then you retrieve the item, and afterward you give a treat, he will know that you are not there simply to steal the thing he has found. Because of the trust that will develop, he will not guard his favorite toys, or food. Negative behaviors, such as guarding, can be avoided with this, and socialization types training.

**Teach "Drop It" Like This**

- Gather a variety of good treats, and a few items your dog might like to chew on, such as a favorite toy, or a rawhide chew. With a few treats in hand, encourage your dog to chew on one of the toys. When the item is in his mouth, *put a treat close to his nose* and say, "drop it!" As soon as he opens his mouth, *click and treat* him as you pick up the item. Then, return the item to your dog.

At this point, your dog may not want to continue to chew on the item because there are treats in the area, and his mouth is now free to consume. If he appears now to be distracted by the treats you possess, rather than the chew-toy, you can take this as an opportunity to pause the training.

Be sure and keep the treats handy though, because throughout the day when you see him pick something up, you both can practice the *drop-it* command. Do this at least ten times per day, or until this command is mastered.

In the event that he picks up a forbidden item you may not want to give back to him, instead, give your puppy an extra tasty treat, or a supersized serving as an equitable exchange for the item that you confiscate. You want your puppy to be redirected, and he should be properly rewarded for his compliance.

- Once you have done the treat-to-the-nose *drop-it* command ten times, try doing it *without* holding the treat to his nose. Continue to use your hand, but this time it should be empty. Say the command, and when he drops the item, *click and treat*. Make sure the first time he drops it, when you are not holding a treat to his nose, that you give him a supersized treat serving from a different hand. Practice this over a few days and training sessions. Do not rush to the next step until his response is consistently compliant, and training is successful.

- This next part of the drop-it training will further reinforce the command, in particular during situations where a tug-of-war between you may ensue. This time you will want to use a treat that your dog might find extra special, like a hard chew pig ear or rawhide, making sure that it is something that cannot be consumed quickly. Next, hold this new chewy in your hand and offer it to your dog, but this time *do not let it go*. When your dog has the chewy in his mouth, say, "drop it." When your dog drops it for the *first time*, C/T, being sure to give your dog extra treats, and then offer the chew back to him to keep.

Because better treats are available, he may not take the chewy back. Recognize this as a good sign, but it also signals a time for a break. Later, repeat this training about a dozen times before you move on to the next phase of "drop it." If your dog is not dropping it after clicking, then the next time use a higher value treat.

- For the next phase of the "drop it" command training, repeat the exercise above, but this time do not hold onto the chew, just let him have it. As soon as your dog has it in his mouth, give the command "drop it." When your dog drops the chewy, C/T a supersized portion, then be sure to give the chew back to him to keep. Your dog will be thrilled by this exchange. Once you have successfully done this a dozen times, move onto the next step.

During this exercise, if your dog does not drop the chewy, it will be necessary to show the treat first, as incentive. Once he realizes that you hold treats, you will want to work up to having him drop-it before the treat is given. This in actuality is *bribery*, and I do not suggest utilizing this action as a short cut elsewhere during training. *Remember,* only use this method as a last resort, and discontinue it quickly.

- Try this command with the things around the house that he is not supposed to chew on, such as pens, chip bags, socks, gloves, tissues, your shoes, or that 15th century Guttenberg bible.

After you and your dog have achieved success indoors with this command, try the exercise outside where there are plenty of distractions. To hold his attention when you are moving into further distracting situations, be sure and have with you the best of treats. Keep in mind that your goal is to have the drop-it command obeyed in any situation.

- Practice the drop-it command when playing fetch, and other games. For example, when your dog returns to you with his ball, command "drop it," and when he complies, offer up the magic duo of praise, plus a treat.

- Gradually phase out the clicking and treating of your dog every time that he drops something on command. Progressively reduce treating by first treating one out of two times, then one out three times, followed by one out of four, five, six, and finally not at all.

Always remain aware of your dog's abilities, and his individual pace, being sure not to decrease treating too rapidly. The desired outcome of this training is that your dog will obey *all* commands by a vocal or physical cue, without a reward.

**Know These Things-**

- If your Westie already likes to try to incite games of grab and chase with you, it is best to curb this behavior from the onset by teaching your dog that you *will not* chase after him if he thieves and bolts. If your dog grabs and runs, *completely* ignore him. For you to be effective here, it means that you do not indicate your disapproval with any sort of eye contact, body language, or vocalization. He will quickly get bored, and drop the item on his own.

- If your dog refuses to drop an item, you may have to retrieve it manually. You can do this by placing your hand over the top of your dog's muzzle, and with your index finger and thumb placed on either side of his upper lip, firmly pinch it into his teeth. Before utilizing this technique, it is best to attempt to calm your dog's excitement as much as possible. In most cases, your dog will open its mouth to avoid the discomfort, and at this time, you can retrieve the item, whatever it may be. This may take a couple of practices to get the correct pressure and the most effective location to apply it.

In the rare instance that this fails, you can simply use both hands and try to separate the jaws by slowly pulling, *not jerking*, the upper and lower jaws apart. Think crocodile handler, minus the severed limbs.

-Another trick for distracting your puppy's attention is by rapping your knuckles on a hard surface, emulating a knock at the door. Often, a puppy will want to investigate what he perceives as a guests arrival, thus dropping whatever is in his mouth to greet the nonexistent visitor.

## ~ *Paws On – Paws Off* ~

# 14  Let's Sit

"Sit" is one of the basic commands that you will use regularly during life with your dog. Teaching your Westie to *sit* establishes human leadership by shaping your dog's understanding of who the boss is. This command can also help curb problem behaviors, such as jumping up on people. It can also assist in teaching polite doggy etiquette, particularly of patiently waiting for you, *the trusted alpha*. Teaching your dog to sit is easy, and a great way for you to work on your catalog of essential alpha behaviors touched upon in previous chapters.

- First, gather treats, then find a quiet place to begin the training. Wait until your puppy sits down by his own will, and soon as his fuzzy rump hits the floor, *click and treat*. Treat your pup while he is still sitting, then promptly get him up and standing again. Continue doing this until your pup immediately sits back down in anticipation of the treat. Each time he complies, be sure to click and treat.

- Next, integrate the verbal command of "sit." Each time he begins to sit on his own, say, "sit," then reinforce with a C/T. From here on, only treat your pup when he sits after being commanded to do so. Practice for 10-15 repetitions then take a break.

**Try these variations for better sitting behavior:**

- Continue the training by adding the distraction of people, animals, and noises to the sessions. As with the come command, you want your dog to sit during any situation that may take place. Practice for at least five minutes each day in places with increasingly more distractions.

- Run around with your dog while you are sharing play with one of his favorite toys. After getting him worked up and excited, command your dog to *sit*. Click and treat your dog when he does.

- Before going outside, delivering food, playing with toys, giving verbal praise, petting, or getting into the car, ask your dog to *sit*. Having your dog sit before setting his food bowl down is something you can practice every day to help bolster his compliance to the sit command.

- Other situations where you can practice the sit command can be when there are strangers present, or before opening doors for visitors. In addition, other excellent opportunities to work on the sit command is when there is food on the table, when you are barbequing, or when you are together in the park.

Keep practicing this command in all situations that you may encounter throughout the day with your dog. I recommend a gradual increase to the level of distraction exposure during this training. Sit is a powerful and indispensable command that you will utilize throughout the life of your dog. Later, we will add the command of "sit-stay" in order to keep your dog in place until you release him.

-It is important eventually to phase out the clicking and treating every time that he obeys the "sit" command. After his consistent obedience to the command, you can begin gradually to reduce C/T by treating every other compliance, then once out three times, followed by once out of four, five, six, and then finally cease. Be sure to observe your dog's abilities and pace, making sure not to decrease C/T too rapidly. The overall goal of this training is to have your dog obey all commands without a reward, and only by a vocal or physical cue.

-Take advantage of each day, and the multiple opportunities you have to practice the sit command.

## *~ Paws On – Paws Off ~*

# 15 "Leave it"

Keep in mind that leave it and drop-it are distinctly different commands. The goal of the *leave it* command is to steer your Westie's attention away from any object before it ends up in his mouth, making it a proactive command.

A proficiency in this command will help to keep him safe from dangerous items, for example objects such as dropped medications, broken glass, trash, wires, chemical tainted rags, or that treasured item you spy your dog about to place into his mouth.

A simple "leave it" command can thwart those especially smelly, frequently dead things that dogs find irresistible and often choose to bring us as offerings of love and affection." We all know that our dogs love to inspect, smell, taste, and in some cases roll in what they find. You can begin to teach the leave it command as soon as your dog recognizes his own name.

- Start with a treat in each fisted hand. Let him have a sniff of one of your fists. When he eventually looks away from the fist and has stopped trying to get the treat, click and treat, but treat your dog from the opposite hand that he sniffed. Repeat this exercise until he completely refrains from trying to get the treat from you, as evidenced by showing no interest in your fist.

- Next, open your hand with the treat, and show him the treat. Close your hand if he tries to get the treat. Do this until he simply ignores the treat in the open hand, known as the decoy hand. When he ignores it, click and give your dog the treat from the other hand. Keep doing this until he ignores the treat in the open hand from the start of the exercise. When you have reached this point, add the command "leave it." Now, open the decoy hand, say "leave it" just once for each repetition, and when your dog does, click and treat him from the other hand.

- Now, put the treat on the floor and say, "leave it." Cover it with your hand if he tries to get it. When your dog looks away from the treat that is lying on the floor, click and treat your dog from the other hand. Continue issuing the command "leave it" until your dog no longer tries to get the treat that is on the floor.

-For the next exercise, put the treat on the floor and say, "leave it," and then stand up. Click and treat if he obeys. Now, walk your dog by the treat while he is on his leash and say, "leave it." If he goes for it, prevent this by restraining him with the leash. C/T him only when he ignores the treat. Increase the length of time between the leave it command and the C/T.

Teaching your dog to leave it using a treat first, will allow you to work up to objects such as toys, animals, pills, spills, and even people. Once he gets the idea in his head that leave it means rewards for him, you both can eventually work towards more complex situations involving more difficult to resist items. Begin with a low value item such as a piece of kibble, then move to a piece of hard to resist meat, his favorite toy, another animal, or people.

- After your dog is successful at leaving alone the treat and other items, take the training outside into the yard, gradually adding people, toys, animals, and other hard to resist distractions. Next, head to the dog park, or any other place with even more distractions.

Remember to keep your puppy clear of dog parks until at least after his seventh week, preferably no sooner than his tenth week, and certainly only after his first round of vaccines. Some veterinarians and experts suggest even waiting until after the second round of vaccinations before your dog is exposed to other animals.

Continue practicing daily until your dog has this command down pat. This is another potential lifesaving command that you will use regularly during the life of your dog.

- At this point, you both can have some real fun. Try placing a dog biscuit on your pups paw, snout, or head and say, "leave it." Gradually increase the time that your pup must leave the biscuit in place. Try this when he is in the sitting and other down positions. Have some fun and be sure to reward your dog the biscuit after he leaves it undisturbed. ~ Enjoy!

- Gradually phase out clicking and treating your dog every time that on command he obeys "leave it." As with prior commands, begin gradually reducing treating by one out of two times, one out three times, then one out of four, five, six, and finally none. Remember not to decrease too quickly or it will undermine your training. Keenly observe your dog's abilities and pace at all times. The goal is that your dog will obey all the commands without a reward, eventually with only a vocal or physical cue.

## ~ *Paws On – Paws Off* ~

# 16 "Down"

Teaching your Westie to lie down not only helps to keep him in one spot, but also offers a calming timeout, in addition, it is a useful intervention to curtail, or even prevent barking. When paired with the stay command, you can keep your dog comfortably in one place for long periods. Down not only protects your dog in potentially hazardous situations, but it also provides you with peace of mind that your dog will remain in the place where you commanded him to stay. This is yet another essential command that you will utilize daily, throughout the lifetime of your dog.

**Basics**

- Begin training in a quiet place with few distractions, and bring plenty of treats. Wait for your dog to lie down of his own will, and then *click and treat* while he is in the lying down position. Toss a treat to get him up again. Repeat this until he begins to lie down immediately after he gets the treat. His compliance means that he is starting to understand that good things come to him when he lies down, so in anticipation of this, he lays right back down.

- Now, augment the training with the addition of the verbal command, "down." As soon as your dog starts to lie down, say "down," and *click and treat*. From here on, only *click and treat* your dog when he lies down after your command.

- Next, practice this in a variety of areas and in situations of various distraction. Begin the practice indoors, then take it outside into your yard, and then wander into the neighborhood, and beyond. Remain patient in the more distracting locations. Situations to command your dog to lie down could be times when there are strangers present, when there is food nearby, or when the stereo or television is on. Anytime you are outdoors barbequing, having a party, in the park, or during your walks together are also excellent opportunities to practice this command. Maintain diligence with this training, and attempt to find situations of increasing levels of distraction where you might need to use the command "down." Remember that consistent compliance is what you are looking for.

The power and importance of the command "down" will prove to be one of the most useful of all to train and maintain during the life of your dog. After your success with the training of "down," you can then move to the combination command of "down-stay," which should be trained in order to keep your dog in place until you release him. Imagine the ease and joy when your pooch accompanies you to the local café, and he lays quietly, as well as *obediently*, at your feet while you drink your morning coffee, or when you eat your meal. Having an obedient companion is a very attractive and respected attribute of any responsible dog owner.

It is important to monitor and track your partner's progress by taking notes during his training, especially as you increase the distractions, highlighting where and when he needs more work, or attention.

- Gradually phase out clicking and treating your dog every time that he obeys the "down" command. Reduce the treats to one time out of two compliances, followed by one out of three, then one out of four, five, six, and finally stop altogether. Do not decrease the treats too rapidly and be sure to observe closely, your dog's abilities and pace. The goal of the training is to have your dog obey *all* commands with only a vocal or physical cue, *without a reward.*

## PROBLEMS SOLVED

- If your dog will not comply with the down command, you need to return the training to a low distraction area, such as a bathroom. Unless your dog likes decorative bath soaps or vanity mirrors, and he may, there is not much to distract him in the bathroom. Continue the training there.

- If your dog does lie down, but pops right back up, be sure that you are only treating him when in the lying down position. In this way, your dog will sooner understand the correlation between the command, action, and the subsequent treat.

### *~ Paws On – Paws Off ~*

# 17 "Stay"

*Stay* is perhaps a command that you have looked forward to teaching, after all, it is up there on top of the list, as one of the most useful and used *essential* commands. This command can be paired with *sit* and *down*. With these combination commands under your belt, daily life with your companion will be made easier.

Teaching your dog restraint has practical uses, as well. By reinforcing the wanted behavior of remaining in place, your dog will not end up in potentially dangerous situations, such as running out the door and into the street. This command also limits the possibility of your dog putting you in embarrassing or inconvenient situations, such as jumping up on people, or chasing the neighbor's pet kangaroo. Furthermore, it is a valuable command that teaches compliance, which facilitates better control of your dog. Stay not only teaches your dog patience, but also reinforces his understanding of who is in charge of the decision-making. After you have taught your dog *sit* and *down*, the stay command should be next on your training agenda, as they make for useful pairings.

- To begin with, find yourselves a quiet low distraction place, and bring plenty of treats. Give the sit command, and after he obeys, wait two-seconds before you *click and treat*. Continue practicing while gradually extending the duration of time between his compliance and his receiving the click and treat, thus reinforcing the length of time he is in the sit position. Work up to 10-15 seconds of sitting before clicking and treating.

- Next, you can begin to issue the combination sit-stay command, and this time you can add a hand signal to the mix. While you issue the command, his signal can simply be your flat hand directed towards his fuzzy little face, at about 12 inches/30 centimeters. You can also choose a unique hand signal of your own to use in conjunction with sit-stay, being careful to avoid the use of the middle finger, as not to offend the neighbors or passersby. Continue practicing while increasing the time he is in the sit position. Gradually increase the sit-stay time to one minute before you C/T.

- If your dog gets up during this training, it means you are moving too quickly. Try again with a shorter stay time goal, and then slowly increase the time your dog is to remain completely still. Continue practicing until your dog will stay for longer intervals. A good way to keep track of your dog's progress through each training session is by starting a training log. This is helpful for many reasons, including monitoring his compliance, goals, outcomes, as well as wanted and unwanted behaviors.

**- Now, it is time to test your progress.**

Now, say "sit-stay," and take one big step away from your dog, then C/T him for his obedience. Keep practicing this until you can take two big steps in any direction, away from your dog without him moving. It is essential that you return to treat your dog at the exact spot in which he stayed in place. Refrain from treating him if he rises, or if he comes to you.

Keep progressing with this exercise until you can take several steps away, eventually moving completely out of sight of your dog, while he stays stationary. Work towards the goal of him staying motionless for two full minutes while you are in his sight, followed by an additional two minutes that you remain out of his sight. By gradually increasing the stay-time interval during this training, you reinforce the stay-response behavior to the point that your dog will stay put *no matter what is going on*. Often dogs will simply lie down after a number of minutes in the stay position. Usually, after about five minutes my dog just lies down until I release him.

- Lastly, begin increasing the distractions, while practicing all that has been trained up to this point. As previously instructed, begin the practice indoors, and then take it outside into the yard, and then move away from the familiarity of your house and neighborhood. For obvious reasons, be patient in the more distracting locations. It is important to maintain a practice routine of at least five minutes per day, particularly in places with increasing distraction. During your training sessions, continue to add other people, animals, all in a variety of noisy and increasingly distracting environments. The desired outcome of this training is to have a dog that remains in place in any situation you both may encounter during your time together.

**Now, repeat the above steps chronologically using the command "*down*."**

- Gradually phase out clicking and treating your dog every time that on command he obeys a command. As previously instructed, phase out treating by reducing it gradually, first by treating one out of two times, then once out three times, followed by once out of four, five, six, and then finally refrain all together. Be sure not decrease the treats too quickly. Observe and take notes of your dog's abilities and pace. The goal is to have a dog that will obey all the commands without reward, and only by a vocal, or physical cue.

When finished with this section you should have the commands "sit-stay" and "down-stay" obeyed by your dog. Take care not to train both commands in the same training sessions.

## HELPFUL HINTS

- *Always* reward your dog in the location where he has remained in place. It is important to refrain from releasing him with a C/T while using the *come* command. This will invariably confuse the outcome of the training, and diminish the importance of the come command. Keep it clear and simple.

- Note when your dog decides not to participate. It could be that the training is getting too difficult, too quickly. Put variation in the stay-time, as well as in the location, when giving commands to your dog. Give the little fella a chance to learn at his own pace.

- Practice the command of *stay,* particularly before he meets a new person. Practice this also before he follows you out the door, or into the car, or in the course of feeding, *before* you put down his food bowl.

- If you encounter any difficulties, back up a step, or calmly resume later. Be aware that each dog has his own pace of learning, so your ongoing patience is crucial. It is best to simply laugh, smile, and roll with your dog's own natural abilities while enjoying the process of teaching and learning together. After all, this is all quality time spent while hanging out with your new best friend.

### ~ *Paws On – Paws Off* ~

# 18  Leash Training

Training your Westie to the leash will probably be one of the hardest things you will do. However, in the end, it is very rewarding and can serve to strengthen the trust and bond between you and your dog. A leash, or lead, is simply the rope that tethers you to your companion. Though a strong, good quality and adjustable leash is key, a feature of greater significance is the collar, or harness. There is a variety of collars to choose from, and it is up to you to do some research to determine which one is best fit for your dog. Head collars and front attachment harnesses are a couple of choices. Make sure it is a good fit and that your dog is comfortable wearing it.

For the sake of your dog's self-esteem, please select one that is stylish and in current fashion. Remember, you don't want the other dogs to stare or tease. On this topic, be sure to keep your eyes peeled for my next book, entitled- *"Doggy Vanity; Styles & Fashion for the Narcissistic Modern Canine."*

Keep in mind some general guidelines suggested when choosing a collar. If you are small and your dog is large, or if your dog tends to be aggressive or powerful, you will need to exert the greatest control, so the sensible choice should be a head collar. Front attachment collars are an excellent choice for any dog or activity. Head and frontal attached collars should be used with leashes with a length of six feet (1.82 meters), or less. The reason for maintaining a shorter leash is that a longer lead length could allow your dog, if he bolts, to gain enough speed to injure himself when the lead runs out and becomes suddenly taut.

The main goal here is to get your dog to walk beside you without pulling against the leash. An effective method during training is simply to stop moving forward when your dog pulls on the lead, turn and walk the opposite direction. Then, when he obediently walks beside you, reward with treats, praise and affection to reinforce the wanted behavior. The following steps will help you train your dog to have excellent leash manners. Remember, *loose leash walking is the goal!*

*Before* moving forward to the next instructional step, please make sure that your dog consistently performs the target action of the training step that you are teaching. His consistent compliance is necessary for the success of this training, so do not be inclined to hurry or rush this training.

**Walking With You Is A Treat** (The beginning)

Start by donning your dog with a standard harness fastened with a non-retractable leash that is about ten to twenty feet (3-6 meters) in length. Before starting the training session, remember to load up your pouch or pockets with top-notch treats and head out to the back yard or another familiar, quiet, low distraction outdoor spot. It is best if there are no other animals or people present during this initial phase.

First, decide whether you want your dog to walk along on your left or right side. It is at this side that you will treat your dog, and when you do, treat at your thigh level. Eventually, your dog will automatically come to that side because that is where the goodies can be found. Later, you can train your dog to walk on either side of you, but for now, stick with one side. In the future, training for both sides allows you the flexibility to maneuver your dog anywhere, whether out of harm's way, or for a more practical application, like easily walking on either side of the street.

- Place a harness or collar on your dog and attach the leash. Begin the training by randomly walking about the yard. When your dog decides to walk along with you, *click and treat* on the chosen side, at the level of your thigh. To "walk along with you" specifically refers to an action where your dog willingly joins you when you move along, in full compliance, and in a manner without applying any resistance to the lead. If he continues to walk on the correct side, and calmly with you, give him a *click and treat* with every step, or two, that you take together, thus reinforcing the desired behavior. Keep practicing this until your dog remains by your side, more often than not.

At this time, do not worry about over-treating your trainee; you will eventually reduce the frequency of delivery, eventually phasing out treats completely upon his successful mastering of this skill. If you are concerned with your companion's waistline, or girlish figure, you can deduct the training treats from the next meal.

- Repeat ambling around the yard with your pal in-tow, but this time walk at a faster pace than your prior session together. As before, when your dog decides to walk with you, give him a *click and treat* at thigh level of the chosen side. Keep practicing this until your dog consistently remains by your side, at this new pace. This leash training should occur over multiple sessions and days.

There is no need to rush any aspects of training. Remember to be patient with all training exercises, and proceed at a pace dictated by your dog's energy level, and his willingness to participate.

**Eyes on the THIGHS** (Second act)

Keeping your dog focused on the training at hand. Teaching him that you are in control of the leash is crucial.

This time, start walking around the yard and wait for a moment when your dog lags behind, or gets distracted by something else. At this time say, "let's go" to him, followed by a non-violent slap to your thigh to get his attention. Make sure you use a cheerful voice when issuing this command, and refrain from any harsh tactics that will intimidate your pooch, which can certainly undermine any training. When he pays attention to you, simply walk away. By doing this, it isolates the cue connected to this specific behavior, thus moving closer to your dog's grasp of the command.

- If your dog catches up with you *before* there is tension on the leash, *click and treat* him from the level of your thigh on the chosen side. *Click and treat* him again after he takes a couple of steps with you, and then continue to reinforce this with a C/T for the next few steps while he continues walking beside you. Remember, the outcome of this training is *loose leash walking*.

If your dog catches up *after* the leash has become taut, *do not treat him*. Begin again by saying, "let's go," then treat him after he takes a couple of steps with you. Only reinforce with C/T when he is compliant.

- If he does not come when you say, "let's go," continue moving until there is tension on the lead. At this point, stop walking and apply firm, but gentle pressure to the leash. When he begins to come toward you, praise him as he proceeds. When he gets to you, *do not treat him*, instead say, "let's go," and begin walking again. Click and treat your dog if he stays with you, and continue to C/T your dog for every step or two that he stays with you.

Keep practicing this step until he remains at your side while you both walk around the yard. If he moves away from you, redirect him with pressure to the lead and command cue of "let's go," followed up with a C/T when he returns to the appropriate position of walking obediently in tandem with you.

Do not proceed forward to subsequent steps of the training until your dog is consistently walking beside you with a loose leash, and is appropriately responding to the "let's go" command. It can sometimes take many days and sessions for your dog to develop this skill, so it is important for you to remain patient and diligent during this time. The outcome of this training is well worth your time and effort.

**Oh! The things to smell and pee on** (Third act)

Just like you, your dog is going to want to sniff things and go potty. During these times, you should be in control. While your dog is on the leash, and when he is in anticipation of his regular treating, or at about each five minute interval, say something like, "go sniff," "go play," "free time," or some other verbal cue that you feel comfortable saying, followed by some self-directed free time on the leash.

Keep in mind that this is a form of reward, but if he pulls on the leash, you will need to redirect with a "let's go" cue, followed by your walking in the opposite direction, quickly ending his free time. If your dog remains compliant, and does not pull on the leash before the allotted free time has elapsed, you are still the one that needs to direct the conclusion of free leash time, by saying, "let's go," coupled with you walking in the opposite direction.

**Where's is my human?** (Fourth act)

Using steps one through three, continue practicing leash walking in the yard. During the course of the training session, gradually shorten the lead until 6-foot (1.8meter) length remains. Now, change the direction and speed of your movements, being sure to *click and treat* your dog every time he is able to stay coordinated with the changes you have implemented.

As loose leashed walking becomes routine and second nature for your companion, you can start phasing out the click and treats. Reserve the C/T for situations involving new or difficult training points, such as keeping up with direction changes, or ignoring potential distractions.

**Out in the Streets** (Fifth act)

Now, it is time to take your dog out of the yard and onto the sidewalk for his daily walk. You will use the same techniques you used in your yard, only now you have to deal with more distractions.

Distractions can come in all forms, including other dogs, friendly strangers, traffic, alarming noises, sausage vendors, feral chickens, taunting cats and a host of other potential interruptions and disturbances. It is during these times that you might want to consider alternate gear, such as a front attachment harness, or a halter collar, which fits over the head offering ultimate control over your companion. Arm yourself with your dog's favorite treats, apply the utmost patience, and go about your walk together in a deliberate and calm manner. Remember to utilize the "let's go," command cue when he pulls against his leash, or forgets that you exist. In this new setting, be sure to treat him when he walks beside you and then supersize the portions if your dog is obedient and does not pull on the lead during a stressful moment, or in an excitable situation. Lastly, do not forget to reward with periodic breaks for sniffing and exploring.

**Stop and Go exercise** (Sixth act)

Attach a 6-foot lead to the collar. With a firm hold on the leash, toss a treat or toy at about twenty feet (6 meters) ahead of you and your dog, then start walking toward it. If your dog pulls the leash and tries to get at the treat, use the "let's go" command and walk in the opposite direction of the treat. If he stays beside you without struggle while you walk toward the treat, allow him have it as a reward.

Practice this several times until your dog no longer pulls toward the treat and stays at your side, waiting for you to make the first move. The other underlying goal is that your dog should always look to you for direction and follow your lead before taking an action such as running after the toy while he is still leashed.

**Switching Sides** (Seventh Act)

After your dog is completely trained to the specific side chosen, and with a few months of successful loose leash walking practice under your belt, then you can begin the training again, targeting the opposing side that the two of you have previously trained towards. There is no need rush, so proceed with the training of the opposite side when you know the time is right, and you are both comfortable with changing it up a bit. As previously mentioned, a dog that is able to walk loose leashed, on either side of you is the desired, target outcome of this training. This skill is essential for navigating your dog, with ease and safety, in the outside world.

**TROUBLE SHOOTING**

- If your dog happens to cross in front of you during your time together, he may be distracted, so it is important to make your presence known to him with a gentle leash tug, or an appropriate command.

- If your dog is lagging behind you, he might be frightened or not feeling well, instead of pulling your dog along, give him a lot of support and encouragement. If the lagging is due to normal behavioral distractions, such as scent sniffing or frequent territorial marking, keep walking along. In this case, it is appropriate to pull gently on the leash to encourage his attention to the task at hand.

- The reinforcement of wanted behaviors necessitates you delivering numerous rewards when your dog walks beside you, or properly executes what it is you are training at that time. During your time together, pay close attention to your dog's moods, patterns and behaviors. You want to pay close attention to these things so that you can anticipate his responses, modify your training sessions, or simply adapt whatever it is you are doing to assure that his needs are being met, and you are both on the same page. Being conscious of your dog's needs will assist in maintaining a healthy, respectful bond between the two of you. Make an effort to use playful tones in your voice, with a frequent "good dog," followed by some vigorous petting, or some spirited play. Try to be aware of when your dog is beginning to tire, and attempt always to end a training session on a high note, with plenty of treats, play, and praise.

**Heel**

You will find this command indispensable when you are out and about, or perhaps when you encounter a potentially dangerous situation. There will be times where you will need to issue a firm command in order to maintain control of your dog in order to keep the both of you out of harms-way. *Heel* is that command.

During your time together exploring the outside world, things such as another aggressive dog, the busy traffic, a construction site, a teasing cat, or that irresistible squirrel may warrant keeping your dog close to you. If trained to the heel command, your dog will be an indispensable asset in helping to avert possible hazardous circumstances. The heel command is a clear instruction, trained to assure that your dog remains close beside you, *until you say otherwise*.

- Begin this training inside of your back yard, or in another low distraction area. First, place a treat in your fist on the side you've decided to train. Let him sniff your fist, then say "heel," followed by a few steps forward, leading him along with the fisted treat at thigh level. Click and treat him as he follows your fist with his nose. The fist is to keep your dog close to you. Practice for a few sessions.

- Next, begin the training as before, but now with an empty fist. With your fist held out in front of you, give the "heel" command, and then encourage your dog follow by your side. When he follows your fist for a couple of steps, *click and treat* him. For each subsequent session, repeat this practice a half dozen times, or more.

- Continue to practice heel while you are moving around, but now begin to increase the length of time *before* you treat your dog. Introduce a new direction in your walking pattern, or perhaps use a serpentine-like maneuver, snaking your way around the yard. You will want to continuously, but progressively challenge him in order to advance his skills, and to bolster his adaptability in various situations.

During all future outings together, this closed-empty-fist will now serve as your non-verbal, physical hand cue instructing your dog to remain in the heel position. From here on out, remember to display your closed-empty-fist at your side when you issue your heel command.

- Now, move the training sessions outside of the security of your yard. The next level of teaching should augment his learning by exposing him to various locations with increasingly more distractions. The implementation of this new variation in training is done to challenge, as well as to enhance your walking companion's adaptability to a variety of situations and stimulus.

Continue to repeat the *heel* command each time you take your dog out on the leash. Keeping his skills fresh with routine practice will ease your mind when out exploring new terrain together. Knowing that your dog will be obedient, and will comply with all of your commands, instructions and cues will be satisfying; in addition, it will keep you both safe and sane.

Out in the crazy, nutty world of ours there are plenty of instances when you will use this command to avoid unnecessary confrontations or circumstances with potentially dangerous outcomes. If by chance you choose to use a different verbal cue other than the commonly used *heel* command, pick a word that is unique, and easy to say, and does not have a common use in everyday language. This way you avoid the possibility for confusion and misunderstanding.

## *~ Paws On – Paws Off ~*

# 19 "Go" West Young Westie

"Go" is a great cue to get your Westie into his crate or onto his mat or rug, and later his *stuffed goose down micro-fiber plush bed*. This is a very handy command to send your dog to a specific location and keep him there while you tend to your business. Before teaching, "go," your dog should already be performing to the commands, *down, stay,* and of course responding to his or her *name*.

While training the following steps, do not proceed to the next step until your dog is regularly performing the current step.

- Find a quiet low distraction location to place a towel or mat on the floor and grab your treats. Put a treat in your hand and use it to lure your dog onto the towel while saying, "Go." When all four paws are on the towel, *click and treat* your dog. Do this about ten to fifteen times.

- Start the same way as above, say "go," but this time have an empty hand, act as though you have a treat in your fist while you are luring your dog onto the mat. When all fours are on the mat *click and treat* your dog. Do this ten to fifteen times.

- Keep practicing with an empty hand and eventually turning the empty hand into a pointed index finger. Point your finger towards the mat. If your dog does not understand, walk him to the mat then click and treat. Do this about ten to fifteen times.

- Now, cue with "go" *while pointing* to the towel, but do not walk to the towel with him. If your dog will not go to the towel when you point and say the command, then keep practicing the step above before trying this step again. Now proceed practicing the command "go" while using the pointed finger and when your dog has all four paws on the mat, click, and then walk over and treat him while he is on the mat. Do this about ten to fifteen times.

- Now, grab your towel and try this on different surfaces and other places, such as grass, tile, patio, carpet, and in different rooms. Continue to practice this in more and more distracting situations and don't forget your towel or mat. Take the mat outdoors, to your friends and families houses, hotel rooms, the cabin, and any other place that you have your trusted companion with you.

**One Step Beyond – "Relax"**

In accordance with "go" This is an extra command you can teach. This is a single word command that encapsulates the command words go, down, and stay all into one word. The purpose is to teach your dog to go to a mat and lie on it until he is released. This is for when you need your dog out from under foot for extended lengths of time, such as when you are throwing a party. Pair it with "down and stay" so your dog will go the mat, lie down, and plan on staying put for an extended period of time. You can substitute your own command, such as "settle," "rest," or "chill," but once you choose a command stick with it and remain consistent.

This command can be used anywhere that you go, letting your dog know that he will be relaxing for a long period and to assume his relaxed posture. You can train this command when your pup is young and it will benefit you and him throughout your life together.

- Place your mat, rug, or what you plan using for your dog to lie.

- Give the "go" command and C/T your dog when he has all four paws on the mat. While your dog is on the mat, issue the command "down stay," then go to him and C/T while your dog is still on the mat.

- Now, give the "relax" command and repeat the above exercise with this "relax" command. Say, "relax," "go" and C/T your dog when he has all four paws on the mat. While your dog is on the mat, issue the command "down stay," and C/T while your dog is still on the mat. When your dog understands the "relax" command it will incorporate go, down, and stay.

Practice 7-10 times per session until your dog is easily going to his mat, lying down, and staying in that position until you release him.

- Next, give only the "relax" command and wait for your dog to go to the mat and lie down *before* you *click and treat* your dog. Do not use any other cues at this time. Continue practicing over multiple sessions, 7-10 repetitions per session, so that your dog is easily following your one word instruction of "relax."

- Now begin making it more difficult; vary the distance, add distractions, and increase the times in the relax mode. This is a wonderful command for keeping your dog out of your way for lengthy durations. You will love it when this command is flawlessly followed.

## HELPFUL HINT

-While you are increasing the time that your dog maintains his relaxed position, click and treat every 5-10 seconds.

- You can also shape this command so that your dog assumes a more relaxed posture than when you issue "down stay." When your dog realizes that the "relax" command encompasses the super relaxed posture that he would normally use under relaxed conditions, he will understand that he will most likely be staying put for a lengthy period and your dog might as well get very comfortable.

Another obedience command that can and should be taught is the release command. Do not forget to teach a release command word to release your dog from any previous command. Release is command #14 in my 49 ½ Dog Tricks book that will soon, or is already for purchase. *Release* is easier to train if your dog already *sits* and *stays* on command.

This command informs your dog that they are free to move from whichever previous command you had issued and your dog complied, such as *sit, down,* and when combined with *stay.* When released your dog should rise from the position but remain in place. This is an obedience command that can keep your dog safe and you from worrying about your dog bolting off or moving at the wrong time during a potentially dangerous situation. You can choose any command, such as "move," or "break." As a reminder, one or two syllable words work best when teaching dogs commands.

## *~ Paws On – Paws Off ~*

# 20 Chewing

All puppies love and enjoy chewing, especially while teething, but a chewing Westie can do some serious damage, so be alert and diligent to thwart that behavior so it does not get out of hand. Keep many toys and doggy chews around so that you can redirect your puppy towards the dog specific toys, and not your new black leather shoes.

Let your pup know that his or her toys are the only acceptable items to be chewed. Loneliness, boredom, fear, teething, and separation anxiety, are feelings that can motivate your puppy into chewing. Until you have trained that *chewing only happens with dog toys*, while you are away you can leave your pup in his crate or gated area. Be sure to throw some dog chew-toys in the crate, limiting his chewing to only those indestructible natural rubber chew-toys.

Lots of physical exercise, training, and mental challenges will assist in steering your dog away from destructive chewing. Until your puppy is over his "I'll chew anything phase," hide your shoes and other items that you do not want chewed, thus temporarily puppy proofing your home. *Puppy proofing* your home entails removing all harmful items that a puppy might chew or swallow, unfortunately, that means everything. Puppies love to put anything into their mouths. After all, they are kids learning about the world. It will be necessary to elevate electrical cords, remove floor debris, and all other random objects that a puppy can chew, eat, or swallow. Thoroughly inspect your entire house that is accessible to your puppy. Apply bitter spray to appropriate furniture and fixed objects that require protection. Take extra caution removing from puppy reach all chemicals, pharmaceuticals, and other toxic liquids that might be accessed around the house.

The "leave it!" command should be trained so you can quickly steer your pup away from anything that is not his to chew. Avoid letting your dog mouth or chew on your fingers or hand, because that can lead to biting behaviors.

## Stuffing Chew-Toys

Steering your puppy towards his chew-toys and away from the off-limits items can be done with the aid of stuffed chew-toys. There are some basic guidelines to follow when using a stuffable chew toy. First, kibble is the recommended foodstuff when filling your puppy's chew-toy. Kibble assists in keeping your puppy at a normal weight, and if this is a concern, you can simply exclude the amount you used in the toy from his normal feeding amount. Secondly, you can use tastier treats, such as cooked meat or freeze-dried liver, but these should be reserved for special rewards. There are plenty of stuffing recipes available, but be cautious about the frequency you treat your puppy with special stuffing. Be conscious of when you reward your puppy, and avoid doing so when bad behaviors are exhibited. For example, if your puppy has been incessantly barking all afternoon, then if you provide a stuffed chew-toy do not reward him with something utterly delectable.

The art to stuffing chew-toys is that the toy holds your puppy's interest, and keeps him occupied. For your success, you will want to stuff the toy in a way that a small portion of food comes out easily, thus quickly rewarding your puppy. After this initial jackpot, the goal is to keep your puppy chewing while gradually being rewarded with small bits of food that he actively extracts. You can use a high value treat, such as a piece of meat stuffed deeply into the smallest hole, which will keep your dog occupied for hours in search of this prized morsel. With a little creativity and practice, the art of chew-toy stuffing will be acquired benefitting you and your canine friend. After trial and error, you will begin to understand what fillings and arrangements will keep your puppy occupied for longer and longer times.

## ~ *Paws On – Paws Off* ~

# 21 Jumping

Your dog loves you and wants as much attention from you as possible. The reality is that you are the world to your dog. Often when your dog is sitting quietly, he is easily forgotten. When he is walking beside you, you are probably thinking about other things, such as work, dinner, the car, chores you need to accomplish, or anything but your loyal companion walking next to you. Sometimes your dog receives your full attention only when he jumps up on you. When your dog jumps up on you, then you look at him, physically react in astonishment, maybe shout at him, and gently push him down until he is down on the floor. Then, you ignore him again, and make a mental note to teach your dog not to jump up onto you. What do you expect? He wants your attention. Teaching your dog not to jump is essentially teaching him that attention will come only if he has all four paws planted firmly on the ground.

It is important not to punish your dog when teaching him not to jump up on you and others. Do not shout "no!" or "bad!" Do not knee your dog or push him down. The best way to handle the jumping is to turn your back and ignore your dog. Remember, since he loves you very much, your dog or puppy may take any physical contact from you as a positive sign. You do not want to send mixed signals; instead, you want to practice complete ignoring that consists of no looking or audio. If you do use a vocal command, do not say, "off," instead use "sit," which your dog has probably already learned. Try not to use a command, and instead proceed with ignoring.

For jumping practice, it would be ideal if you could gather a group of people together who will participate in helping you train your dog that jumping is a no-no. You want to train your dog to understand that he will only get attention if he is on the ground. If groups of people are not available, then teach him to remain grounded using his family. When your dog encounters other people, use a strong "sit stay" command to keep all four paws planted firmly on the ground. I covered "sit stay" above, and now you understand how useful and versatile this command can be.

## No Jumping On the Family

This is the easiest part, because the family and frequent visitors have more chances to help your dog or puppy to learn. When you come in from outside and your dog starts jumping up, say, "oops!" or "whoa," and immediately leave through the same door. Wait a few seconds after leaving and then do it again. When your dog finally stops jumping upon you as you enter, give him a lot of attention. Ask the rest of the family to follow the same protocol when they come into the house. If you find that he is jumping up at other times as well, like when you sing karaoke, walking down the hallway, or are cooking at the barbeque, just ignore your dog by turning your back and put energy into giving him attention when he is sitting.

## No Jumping on Others

Prevention is of utmost importance and the primary focus in this exercise, especially with larger dogs. You can prevent your dog from jumping by using a leash, a tieback, crate, or gate. Until you have had enough practice and your dog knows what you want him to do, you really should use one of these methods to prevent your dog from hurting someone or getting an inadvertent petting reward for jumping. To train, you will need to go out and solicit some dog training volunteers and infrequent visitors to help.

- Make what is called a *tieback*, which is a leash attached to something sturdy, within sight of the doorway but not blocking the entrance keeping your dog a couple of feet or about a meter away from the doorway. Keep this there for a few months during the training period until your dog is not accosting you or visitors. When the guest arrives, hook your dog to the secure leash and then let the guest in.

## Guests Who Want to Help Train Your Dog (Thank you in advance)

All of these training sessions may take many sessions to complete, so remain patient and diligent in training and prevention until your dog complies with not jumping on people.

- Begin at home, and when a guest comes in through the door, and the dog jumps up, they are to say "oops" or "whoa," and leave immediately. Practice this with at least five or six different visitors, each making multiple entrances during the same visit. If your helpers are jumped, have them completely ignore your dog by not making any eye contact, physical or vocal actions other than the initial vocal word towards your dog, then have them turn their backs and immediately leave.

- When you go out onto the streets, have your dog leashed. Next, have your guest helper approach your dog. If he strains against the leash or jumps have the guest turn their back and walk away. When your dog calms himself and sits, have the guest approach again. Repeat this until the guest can approach, pet and give attention to your dog without your dog jumping up. Have the volunteer repeat this at least five to seven times. Remember to go slowly and let your dog have breaks. Keep the sessions in the 5-7 minute range. For some dogs, this type of training can get frustrating. Eventually, your dog will understand that his jumping equals being ignored.

- Use the tie-back that you have placed near the door. Once your dog is calm, the visitor can greet your dog if they wish. If the guest does not wish to greet your dog, give your dog a treat to calm his behavior. If he barks, send your dog to his crate or the gated time out area. The goal is that you always greet your guests first, *not your dog*. Afterward, your guests have the option to greet or not greet, instead of your dog always rushing in to greet every guest. If he is able to greet guests calmly while tied back, then he may be released. At first hold the leash to see how your dog reacts, then if he is calm release him.

**A Caveat to These Two Methods**

1) For those who are not volunteers to help teach your dog and are at your home visiting, there is another method. Keep treats by the door, and as you walk in throw them seven to nine feet (2.1 - 2.7 meters) away from you. Continue doing this until your dog begins to anticipate this. Once your dog is anticipating treats every time someone comes through the door it will keep him from accosting you or visitors that walk through the doorway. After your dog eats his treat and he has calmed down a bit, ask him to sit, and then give him some good attention.

2) Teach your dog that a hand signal such as grabbing your left shoulder means the same as the command "sit." By combining the word "sit" with a hand on your left shoulder, he will learn this. If you want to use another physical cue, you can substitute your own gesture here, such as holding your left wrist or ear.

Ask the guests that have volunteered to help train your dog to place their right hand on their left shoulders and wait until your dog *sits* before they pet him or give any attention. Training people that meet your dog will help both you and your dog in preventing unwanted excitement and jumping up. Having your dog sit before he can let loose with jumps is proactive jumping prevention.

## ~ *Paws On – Paws Off* ~

# 22  Barking

Any dog owner knows that dogs bark for many reasons, most commonly, for attention. Your Westie may bark for play, attention, or because it is close to feeding time and he wants you to feed him. Dogs also bark to warn intruders and us, so we need to understand why our dog is barking. Not all barking is bad. Some dogs are short duration barkers, and others can go on for hours, we do not want that and either do our neighbors.

Whatever the case *do not* give your dog attention for barking. Do not send the signals that your dogs barking gets an immediate reaction from you, such as you coming to see why he is barking or moving towards him. As I mentioned in the opening paragraph, they do sometimes bark to warn us, so we should not ignore all barking, we need to assess the barking situation before dismissing it as nonsense barking.

When you know the cause is a negative behavior that needs correction, say, "leave it" and ignore him. While not looking at your dog go to the other side of the room, or into another room, you can even close the door behind you until your dog has calmed down. Make it clear to your barking dog that his barking does not result in any rewards or attention.

In everyday life, make sure you are initiating activities that your dog enjoys and always happening on *your* schedule. You are the alpha leader so regularly show your pup who is in charge. Also, make sure that he earns what he is provided. Have your pup *sit* before he gets any reward.

Your dog may bark when seeing or hearing something interesting. Below are a few ways to deal with this issue.

**Prevention when you are at your residence**

- *Teach your dog the command "quiet."* When your dog barks, wave a piece of food in front of his nose at the same time you are saying, "quiet." When he stops barking to sniff, *click and treat* him right away. Do this about four or five times. Then the next time he barks, pretend you have a piece of food in your hand next to his nose and say, "quiet." Always *click and treat* him as soon as he *stops* barking. After issuing the "quiet" command, *click and treat* him again for every few seconds that he remains quiet.

Eventually, as you make your way to five or ten seconds, gradually increase the time duration between the command "quiet," and *clicking and treating*.

- *Prevent it.* Block the source of sound or sight so that your dog is unable to see or hear the catalyst that is sparking his barking. Use a fan, stereo, TV, curtains, blinds, or simply put him in a different area of the house to keep him away from the stimulus.

- When your pup hears or sees something that would typically make him bark and he *does not bark*, reward him with attention, play, or a treat. This is reinforcing and shaping good behaviors instead of negative behaviors.

**The Time Out**

- Yes you can you can use a *time out* on your dog, but do not use it too often. When you give your dog a time out, you are taking your dog out of his social circle and giving your dog what is known as a negative punishment.

This kind of punishment is powerful and can have side effects that you do not want. Your dog may begin to fear you when you walk towards him, especially if you have the irritated look on your face that he recognizes as the *time out face*. The *time out* should be used sparingly. Instead, focus on teaching your dog the behaviors that you prefer while preventing the bad behavior.

Choose a place where you want the time out spot to be located. Make sure that this place is not the relief spot, crate, or his play area. Ideally it is a boring place that is somewhere that is not scary, not too comfortable, but safe. A gated pantry or the bathroom can work well.

Secure a 2-foot piece of rope or a short leash to your puppy's collar. When your pup barks, use a calm voice and give the command, "time out," then take the rope and walk him firmly but gently to the time out spot. Leave him there for about 5 minutes, longer if necessary. When your dog is calm and not barking, release him. You may need to do this two to a dozen times before he understands which behavior has put him into the time out place. Most dogs are social and love being around their humans, so this can have a strong impact.

**Prevention when you are away from your residence**

- Again, prevent barking by blocking the sounds or sights that are responsible for your dog or puppy going into barking mode. Use a fan, stereo, curtain, blinds, or keep him in another part of the house away from the stimulus.

- Use a Citronella Spray Collar. Only use this for when the barking has become intolerable. Do not use this when the barking is associated with fear or aggression. You will want to use this a few times when you are at home, so that your dog understands how it works.

Citronella collars work like this. The collar has a sensitive microphone, which senses when your dog is barking, when this happens it triggers a small release of citronella spray into the area above a dog's nose. It surprises the dog and disrupts barking by emitting a smell that dogs dislike.

**Out walking**

While you are out walking your dog, out of shear excitement or from being startled, he might bark at other dogs, people, cars, and critters. This can be a natural reaction or your dog may have sensitivities to certain tones, the goal is to try to limit the behavior and quickly cease the barking.

### *Here are some helpful tools to defuse that behavior.*

- Teach your dog the *"watch me"* command. Begin this training in the house in a low distraction area. While you hold a treat to your nose, say your dog's name and "watch me." When your dog looks at the treat for at least one second give him a click and treat. Repeat this about 10-15 times. Then increase the time that your dog looks at you to 2-3 seconds, and repeat a dozen times.

- Then, repeat the process while pretending to have a treat on your nose. You will then want to incorporate this hand to your nose as your hand signal for *watch me*. *Click and treat* when your dog looks at you for at least one second, then increase to two or three seconds, and *click and treat* after each goal. Repeat this about 10-15 times.

- Increase the duration that your dog will continue to watch you while under the command. Click and treat as you progress. Try to keep your dog's attention for 5-10 seconds. Holding your dog's attention for this length of time usually results in the catalyst for him to move away from the area or to lose interest.

- Now, practice the "watch me" command while you are walking around inside the house. Then practice this again outside. When outside, practice near something he finds interesting. Practice in a situation that he would normally bark. Continue practicing in different situations and around other catalysts that you know will produce your dog barking.

This is a great way to steer attention towards you and away from your dog's barking catalysts.

**Other Solutions**

- When you notice something that normally makes your dog bark and he has not begun to bark, use the "quiet" command. For example, your dog regularly barks at the local skateboarder. When the trigger that provokes your dog's barking, the skateboarder comes zooming by, use the command "quiet," and *click and treat*. Click and treat your dog for every few seconds that he remains quiet. Teach your dog that his barking trigger gets him a "quiet" command. Your dog will begin to associate the skateboarder with treats and gradually it will diminish his barking outbursts at the skateboarder.

- If he frequently barks while a car is passing by, put a treat by his nose, and then bring it to your nose. When he looks at you, *click and treat* him. Repeat this until he voluntarily looks at you when a car goes by and does not bark, continuing to *treat* him appropriately.

- You can also reward your dog for calm behavior. When you see something or encounter something that he would normally bark at and he does not, *click and treat* your dog. *Instead of treats, sometimes offer praise and affection.*

- If you are out walking and your dog has not yet learned the *quiet* cue, or is not responding to it, turn around and walk away from whatever is causing your dog to bark. When he calms down, offer a reward.

- As a last resort use the citronella spray collar if your dogs barking cannot be controlled using the techniques that you have learned. Use this only when the barking is *not* associated with fear or aggression.

**Your dog is Afraid, Aggressive, Lonely, Territorial, or Hung-over**

Your dog may have outbursts when he feels territorial, aggressive, lonely, or afraid. All of these negative behaviors can be helped with proper and early socialization, but occasionally they surface. Many times rescue dogs might have not been properly socialized and bring their negative behaviors into your home. Be patient while you are teaching your new dog proper etiquette. Some breeds, especially watch and guarding breeds are prone to territorialism and it can be a challenge to limit their barking.

- This is not a permanent solution, but is a helpful solution while you are teaching your dog proper barking etiquette. To allow your dog a chance to find his center, relax his mind and body, do this for about seven to ten days before beginning to train against barking. As a temporary solution, you should first try to prevent outbursts by crating, gating, blocking windows, using fans or music to hide sounds, and avoid taking your dog places that can cause these barking outbursts.

**SOME TIPS**

- Always, remain calm, because a relaxed and composed alpha achieves great training outcomes. A confident, calm, cool, and collected attitude that states you are unquestionably in charge goes a long way in training.

- If training is too stressful or not going well, you may want to hire a professional positive trainer for private sessions. When interviewing, tell him or her that you are using a clicker and rewards based training system and are looking for a trainer that uses the same type or similar methods.

It is important to help your dog to modify his thinking about what tends to upset him. Teach him that what he was upset about before now predicts his favorite things. Here is how.

- When the trigger appears in the distance, *click and treat* your dog. Keep clicking and treating your dog as the two of you proceed closer to the negative stimulus.

- If he is territorially aggressive, teach him that the doorbell or a knock on the door means that is his cue to get into his crate and wait for treats. You can do this by ringing the doorbell and luring your dog to his crate and once he is inside the crate giving him treats.

- You can also lure your dog through his fears. If you are out walking and encounter one of his triggers, put a treat to his nose and lead him out and away from the trigger zone.

- Use the "watch me" command when you see him getting nervous or afraid. *Click and treat* him frequently for watching you.

- Reward *calm* behavior with praise, toys, play, or treats.

- *For the hangover, I recommend lots of sleep.*

**Your dog is frustrated, bored or both**

All dogs including your dog or puppy may become bored or frustrated. At these times, your dog may lose focus, not pay attention to you, and *spend time writing bad poetry in his journal*. Here are a few things that can help prevent this:

- Keep him busy and tire him out with chew toys, exercise, play, and training. These things are a cure for most negative behaviors. A tired dog is usually happy to relax and enjoy quiet time.

- He should have at least 30 minutes of aerobic exercise per day. In addition to the aerobic exercise, each day he should have an hour of chewing and about 15 minutes of training. Keep it interesting for him with a variety of activities. It is, after all, the spice of life.

- Use the command "quiet" or give your dog a time out.

- As a last resort, you can break out the citronella spray collar.

**Excited to Play**

- Like an actor in the wings, your puppy will get excited about play. Teach your dog that when he starts to bark, the playtime stops. Put a short leash on him and if he barks, use it to lead him out of play sessions. Put your dog in a time out or just stop playing with your dog. Reward him with more play when he calms down.

Armed with these many training tactics to curb and stop barking, you should be able to gradually reduce your dogs barking, and help him to understand that some things are not worth barking. Gradually you will be able to limit the clicking and treating, but it is always good practice to reward your dog for not barking. Reward your dog with supersized treat servings for making the big breakthroughs.

## ~ *Paws On – Paws Off* ~

# 23 Nipping

Friendly and feisty, little puppies nip for a few reasons; they are teething, playing or they want to get your attention. *My Uncle Jimmy nips from a bottle, but that is a completely different story.* If you have acquired yourself a nipper, not to worry, in time most puppies will grow out of this behavior on their own. Other dogs, such as some of those bred for herding, nip as a herding instinct. They use this behavior to round up their animal charges, other animals, family members, including those who are *human*.

While your dog is working through the nipping stage, you will want to avoid punishing or correcting your dog because this could eventually result in a strained relationship down the road. However, you will want to teach your puppy how delicate human skin is. Let your dog test it out and give him feedback. You can simply indicate your discomfort when he bites too hard, by using and exclamation, such as, *"yipe!"*, *"youch!"*, or *"Bowie!"* This in addition to a physical display of your pain by pulling back your hand, calf or ankle, will usually be enough for your dog to understand that it is not an acceptable behavior.

After this action, it is important to cease offering any further attention towards your dog, because this offers the possibility that the added attention will reinforce the negative behavior. If you act increasingly more sensitive to the nips, he will begin to understand that we humans are very sensitive, and will quickly respond with a sudden vocal and physical display of discomfort.

This is a very easy behavior to modify because we know the motivation behind it. The puppy wants to play and chew, and who is to blame him for this? Remember, it is important to give your dog access to a variety of chew-toys, and when he nips, respond accordingly, then immediately walk away and ignore him. If he follows you, and nips at your heels, give your dog a time out. Afterward, when your dog is relaxed, calm and in a gentle disposition, stay and play with him. Use the utmost patience with your puppy during this time, and keep in mind that this behavior will eventually pass.

Herding dogs will not so easily be dissuaded, though. For these breeds, it is not always possible to curb this behavior entirely, but you can certainly limit or soften it, eventually making them understand that nipping humans is a *no-no*, and *very painful*. To address this more thoroughly, between the ages of four to five months herding dogs can be enrolled in behavioral classes. This will reinforce your training and boost what you are training at home.

**Preventing the "Nippage"**

- Always have a chew toy in your hand when you are playing with your puppy. This way he learns that the right thing to bite and chew is the toy, and is *not your hands, or any other part of your body.*

- Get rid of your puppy's excess energy by exercising him *at least* an hour each day. As a result, he will have no energy remaining to nip.

- Make sure he is getting adequate rest and that he is not cranky from lack of sleep. Twelve hours per day is good for dogs, and it seems for teenagers as well.

- Always have lots of interesting chew toys available to help your puppy to cope during the teething process.

- Teach your kids not to run away screaming from nipping puppies. They should walk away quietly, or simply stay still. Children should never be left unsupervised when around dogs.

- Play with your puppy in his gated puppy area. This makes it easier to walk away if he will not stop biting or mouthing you. This quickly reinforces his understanding that hard bites end play sessions.

- As a last resort, when the other interventions and methods discussed above are not working, you should increase the frequency of your use of a tieback to hold your dog in place, within a gated or time out area. If your dog is out of control with nipping or biting, and you have not yet trained him that biting is an unacceptable behavior, you may have to use this method until he is fully trained. For example, you may want to use this when guests are over, or if you simply need a break. Always use a tieback while your dog is under supervision, and never leave him tied up alone. The tieback is a useful method and can be utilized as a tool of intervention when addressing other attention getting behaviors like jumping, barking, and the dreaded leg humping.

The best option during this time, early in his training, is to place him in a room with a baby gate in the doorway.

**Instructing Around the "Nippage"**

- Play with your dog and praise him for being gentle. When he nips say, "*yipe!*" mimicking the sound of an injured puppy, and then immediately walk away. After the nipping, wait one minute and then return to give him another chance at play, or simply remain in your presence *without nipping*. Practice this for two or three minutes, remembering to give everyone present or those who will have daily contact with him a chance to train him through play. It is crucial that puppies *do not receive any reward for nipping*. After an inappropriate bite or nip, all physical contact needs to be abruptly stopped, and quick and complete separation needs to take place so that your puppy receives a clear message.

- After your puppy begins to understand that bites hurt, and if he begins to give you a softer bite, *continue to act hurt, even if it doesn't*. In time, your dog will understand that only the slightest pressures by mouth are permissible during play sessions. Continue practicing this until your puppy is only using the softest of mouths, and placing limited tension upon your skin.

- Next, the goal is to decrease the frequency of mouthing. You can use the verbal cues of *quit* or *off* to signal that his mouth needs to release your appendage. Insist that the amount of time your puppy uses his mouth on you needs to decrease in duration, as well as the severity of pressure needs to decrease. If you need incentive, use kibble or liver to *reward after you command and he obeys*. Another reward for your puppy when releasing you from his mouth grasp is to give him a chew or chew-toy stuffed with food.

- The desired outcome of this training is for your puppy to understand that mouthing any human, if done at all, should be executed with the utmost care, and in such a manner, that without question the pressure *will not inflict pain or damage*.

- Continue the training using the verbal cue of *quit*, until *quit* becomes a well-understood command, and your dog consistently complies when it is used. Interject breaks every 20-30 seconds when playing and any type of mouthing is occurring. The calm moments will allow excitement to wane, and will help to reduce the chances of your dog excitably clamping down. Practice this frequently, and as a part of your regular training practice schedule. The result from successful training and knowing that your dog will release upon command will give you piece of mind.

- If you have children, or are worried about the potential for injury due to biting, you can continue training in a way that your dog knows that mouthing is *not permitted under any circumstance*. This level of training permits you from having to instruct a permissible mouthing pressure. This will result in a reduction of your anxiety whenever your dog is engaged in playing with your family or friends. This of course nearly eliminates the potential for biting accidents to occur.

Remain vigilant when visitors are playing with your dog. Monitor the play, and be especially attentive to the quality of the interaction, being alert that the session is not escalating into a rough and potentially forceful situation in which your dog might choose to use his mouth in an aggressive or harmful way.

You will need to decide the rules of engagement, and it will be your responsibility that others understand these rules. To avoid harm or injury it will be necessary for you to instruct visitors and family prior to play.

### ~ *Paws On – Paws Off* ~

# 24 Digging Help

Some dogs are going to dig no matter what you do to stop it. For these diggers like the Westie, this behavior is bred into them, so remember that these dogs have an urge to do what they do. Whether this behavioral trait is for hunting or foraging, it is deeply imbedded inside their DNA and it is something that cannot be turned off easily, or at all. Remember that when you have a digger for a dog, they will tend to be excellent escape artists, so you will need to bury your perimeter fencing deep to keep them inside your yard or kennel.

Cold weather dogs such as Huskies, Malamutes, Chows, and other "Spitz" type dogs often dig a shallow hole in an area to lie down in, to either cool down, or warm up. These dogs usually dig in a selected and distinct area, such as in the shade of a tree or shrub.

Other natural diggers such as Terriers, and Dachshunds, are natural hunters and dig to bolt or hold prey at bay for their hunting companions. These breeds have been genetically bred for the specific purpose of digging into holes to chase rabbits, hare, badgers, weasels, and other burrowing animals. Scenthounds such as Beagles, Bassets, and Bloodhounds will dig under fences in pursuit of their quarry. This trait is not easily altered or trained away, but you can steer it into the direction of your choosing. To combat dog escapes you will need to bury your fencing or chicken wire deep into the ground. It is suggested that 18-24 inches, or 46-61cm into the soil below the bottom edge of your fencing is sufficient, but we all know that a determined dog may even go deeper, when in pursuit of quarry. Some dog owners will affix chicken wire at about 12 inches (30.5cm) up onto the fence, and then bury the rest down deep into the soil. Usually, when the digging dog reaches the wire, its efforts will be thwarted and it will stop digging.

Some dogs dig as an instinctive impulse to forage for food to supplement their diet. Because dogs are omnivorous, they will sometimes root out tubers, rhizomes, bulbs, or any other edible root vegetable that is buried in the soil. Even nuts buried by squirrels, newly sprouting grasses, the occasional rotting carcass or other attractive scents will be an irresistible aroma to their highly sensitive noses.

Other reasons dogs dig can be traced directly to boredom, lack of exercise, lack of mental and physical stimulation, or improperly or under-socialized dogs. Improperly socialized dogs can suffer from separation anxiety and other behavioral issues. Non-neutered dogs may dig an escape to chase a female in heat. Working breeds such as Border Collies, Australian Cattle Dogs, Shelties, and other working breeds can stir up all sorts of trouble if not kept busy. This trouble can include incessant digging.

It has been said that the smell of certain types of soil can also catch a dog's fancy. Fresh earth, moist earth, certain mulches, topsoil, and even sand are all lures for the digger. If you have a digger, you should fence off the areas where you are using these alluring types of soils. These kinds of soils are often used in newly potted plants or when establishing a flowerbed or garden. The smell of dirt can sometimes attract a dog that does not have the strong digging gene, but when he finds out how joyful digging can be, beware; you can be responsible for the creation of your own "Frankendigger."

Proper socialization, along with plenty of mental and physical exercises will help you in your fight against digging, but as we know, some diggers are going to dig no matter what the situation. Just in case your dog or puppy is an earnest excavator, here are some options to help you curb that urge.

**The Digging Pit**

A simple and fun solution is to dig a pit specifically for him or her to dig to their little heart's content. Select an appropriate location, and with a spade, turn over the soil a bit to loosen it up, mix in some sand to keep it loose as well as to improve drainage, then surround it with stones or bricks to make it obvious by sight that this is the designated spot.

To begin training your dog to dig inside the pit, you have to make it attractive and worth their while. First bury bones, chews, or a favorite toy, then coax your dog on over to the pit to dig up some treasures. Keep a watchful eye each time you bring your dog out, and do not leave him or her unsupervised during this training time. It is important to halt immediately any digging outside of the pit. When they dig inside of the designated pit, be sure to reward them with treats and praise. If they dig elsewhere, direct them back to the pit. Be sure to keep it full of the soil-sand mixture, and if necessary, littered with their favorite doggie bootie. If your dog is not taking to the pit idea, an option is to make the other areas where they are digging temporarily less desirable such as covering them with chicken wire, and then making the pit look highly tantalizingly, like a *doggie digging paradise.*

## Buried Surprises

Two other options are leaving undesirable surprises in the unwanted holes your dog has begun to dig. A great deterrent is to place your dog's own *doodie* into the holes that he has dug, and when your dog returns to complete his job, he will not enjoy the gift you have left him, thus deterring him from further digging.

Another excellent deterrent is to place an air-filled balloon inside the hole and then cover it with soil. When your dog returns to his undertaking and then his little paws burst the balloon, the resulting loud "POP!" sound will startle, and as a result, your dog will reconsider the importance of his or her mission. After a few of these shocking noises, you should have a dog that thinks twice before digging up your bed of pansies.

## Shake Can Method

This method requires a soda can or another container filled with rocks, bolts, or coins, remembering to place tape or apply the cap over the open end to keep the objects inside. Keep this "rattle" device nearby so that when you let your dog out into the yard you can take it with you to your clandestine hiding spot. While hidden out of sight, simply wait until our dog begins to dig. Immediately at the time of digging, take that can of coins and shake it vigorously, thereby startling your dog. Repeat the action each time your dog begins to dig, and after a few times your dog should refrain from further soil removal. Remember, the goal is to *startle* and to distract your dog at the time they initiate their digging, and not to terrorize your little friend.

## Shake can instructions

1. Shake it quickly once or twice then stop. The idea is to make a sudden and disconcerting noise that is unexpected by your dog who is in the process of digging. If you continue shaking the can, it will become an ineffective technique.

2. Beware not to overuse this method. Remember your dog *can become desensitized* to the sound, and thus ignore the prompt.

3. Sometimes, it is important to supplement this method by using commands, such as "No" or "Stop."

4. Focus these techniques, targeting only the behavior (e.g. digging) that you are trying to eliminate.

5. Sometimes, a noise made by a can with coins inside may not work, but perhaps using a different container filled with nuts and bolts, or other items will. Examples are soda or coffee cans that are filled with coins, nuts, bolts, or other metal objects. You might have to experiment to get an effective and disruptive sound. If the noise you make sets off prolonged barking instead of a quick startled bark, then the sound is obviously not appropriate. If your dog does begin to bark after you make the noise, use the "quiet" command immediately after, and never forget to reward your dog when he or she stops the barking, thereby reinforcing the wanted behavior.

I hope that these methods will assist you in controlling or guiding your four-legged landscaper in your desired direction. Anyone that has had a digger for a dog knows it can be challenging. Just remember that tiring them out with exercise and games is often the easiest and most effective in curbing unwanted behaviors.

*~ Paps*

**~ *Paws On – Paws Off ~***

# PART III

# 25 Body Language and Vocals

Training your dog seems like a daunting task, but it is a unique and rewarding experience. It is the foundation of a healthy and long relationship with your new dog or puppy. You must be the one in charge of the relationship and lead with the pack leader mentality, all the while showing patience and love. Whether you choose to enroll your dog in an obedience school such as the Sirius™ reward training system or go it alone at home, you will the need assistance of quality books, videos, and articles to help guide you through the process and find solutions to obstacles along the way.

Without a doubt, it is nice to have an obedient friend by your side through good times and bad. Owning a dog is a relationship that needs tending throughout the years. Once you begin training, it will continue throughout the life of your dog and friend. An obedient dog is easier to care for and causes less household problems and expense. You know what needs to be done, but what about your dog. How do you read his messages in regards to what you are attempting to accomplish? I am going to cover dog's body language and vocal language to provide insight into what it is your dog is trying to tell you. This should prove to be an asset while training your dog.

Remember that we cannot always read a dog's body language accurately. All dogs have their own unique personality; therefore will express themselves in their individual way. It is possible that a dog's happy wagging tail could be another dog's way of conveying that it is nervous or anxious. Keep in in your thoughts when reading a dog's body language that it is difficult to be 100% accurate interpreting and to use caution around strange dogs.

## Body Language

What is body language? Body language is all of the non-verbal communication we exhibit when engaged into an exchange with another entity. Say what? All of those little tics, spasms, and movements that we act out comprise of non-verbal body language. Studies state that over 50% of how people judge us is based on our use of body language. Apparently, the visual interpretation of our message is equal to our verbal message. It is interesting how some studies have indicated that when the body language disagrees with the verbal, our verbal message accounts for as little as 7-10% of how the others judge us. With that kind of statistic, I would say that body language is extremely important.

Similar to humans, dogs use their bodies to communicate. Their hearing and seeing senses are especially acute. Observe how your dog tilts his head, moves his legs, and what is his tail doing while you are engaged. Is the tail up, down, or wagging? These body movements are all part of the message your dog is trying to convey. With this knowledge, I think it is safe to say that we should learn a little about human and dog body language. In this article, I will stick to a dog's body language and leave the human investigation up to you. What do you think my posture is right now?

## The Tail

The tail is a wagging and this means the dog is friendly, or maybe not. With most dogs that have tails it can convey many messages, some nice, some nasty. Specialists say a dog's wagging tail can mean the dog is scared, confused, preparing to fight, confident, concentrating, interested, or happy. Some dogs have curly spitz type tails and therefore it will take a keen eye to see and denote what their tail position might be conveying so you will have to rely more on facial and body postures. Breeds with docked tails, flat faces, and that are black in color make it more difficult to read what they are trying express. From distance black colored dogs facial expressions can be difficult to see. Creating further difficulties are breeds that have puffy hair, long hair, or extensive hair that hides their physical features.

How do you tell the difference? Look at the speed and range of motion in the tail. The wide-fast tail wag is usually the message of "Hey, I am so happy to see you!" wag. The tail that is not tight between the hind legs, but instead is sticking straight back horizontally means the dog is curious but unsure, and probably not going to bite but remain in a place of neutral affection. This dog will probably not be confrontational, yet the verdict is not in. The slow tail wag means the same; the dog's friendly meter is gauging the other as friend or foe.

The tail held high and stiff, or bristling (hair raised) is a WATCH OUT! - Red Flag warning for humans to be cautious. This dog may not only be aggressive, but dangerous and ready to rumble. If you come across this dog, it is time to calculate your retreat and escape plan.

Not only should the speed and range of the wag be recognized while you are reading doggie body language, one must also take note of the tail position. A dog that is carrying its tail erect is a self-assured dog in control of itself. On the flip side of that, the dog with their tail between their legs, tucked in tight is the, "I surrender man, I surrender, please don't hurt me" posture.

The chill dog, a la Reggae special is the dog that has her tail lowered but not tucked in-between her legs. The tail that is down and relaxed in a neutral position states, the dog is relaxed.

While training your dog or simply playing, it is a good idea to take note of what his or her tail is doing and determine if your dog's tail posture is matching their moods. Your understanding of your dog's tail movements and body posture will be of great assistance throughout its lifetime.

## Up Front

On the front end of the dog is the head and ears with their special motions. A dog that cocks his head or twitches her ears is giving the signal of interest and awareness, but sometimes it can indicate fear. The forward or ear up movements can show a dog's awareness of seeing or hearing something new. Due to the amazingly acute canine sense of hearing, this can occur long before we are aware. These senses are two of the assets that make dogs so special and that make them fantastic guard and watchdogs.

"I give in, and will take my punishment" is conveyed with the head down and ears back. Take note of this submissive posture, observe the neck, and back fur for bristling. Sometimes this accompanies this posture. Even though a dog is giving off this submissive stance, it should be approached with caution because it may feel threatened and launch an offensive attack thinking he needs to defend himself.

"Smile, you are on camera." Yep, you got it, dogs smile too. It is usually a subtle corner pull back to show the teeth. Do not confuse this with the obvious snarl that entails a raised upper lip and bared teeth, sometimes accompanied by a deep growling sound. The snarl is something to be extremely cautious of when encountered. A snarling dog is not joking around--*the snarl is serious*. This dog is ready to be physically aggressive.

## The Whole Kit and Caboodle

Using the entire body, a dog that rolls over onto its back and exposes his belly, neck, and genitals is conveying the message that you are in charge. A dog that is overly submissive sometimes urinates a small amount to express his obedience towards a human or another dog.

Front paws down, rear end up, tail is a waggin.' This, "hut, hut, hut, C'mon Sparky hike the ball," posture is the ole K-9 position of choice for, "Hey! It is playtime, and I am ready to go!" This posture is sometimes accompanied with a playful bark and or pawing of the ground in an attempt to draw you into his playful state. I love it when a dog is in this mood, albeit they can be aloof to commands.

## Whines, Growls, Howls, Barks and Yelps. Sounds dogs make and we hear

We just had a look at the silent communication of body language. Now, I will look into the doggie noises we cherish, but sometimes find annoying. Just what is our dog trying to tell us? Our canine friends often use vocal expressions to get their needs met. Whines and growls mean what they say, so when training your dog, listen carefully. As you become accustomed to the dogs vocal communication, and are able to begin understanding them, the happier you will both become. Some dog noises can be annoying and keep you awake, or wake you up. This may need your attention, to be trained out as inappropriate vocalizations.

## Barking

What does a dog bark say and why bark at all? Dogs bark to say "Hey, what's up dude," "I am hungry," or "Look at me!" A bark may warn of trouble, or to convey that the dog is bored or lonely. I think we all know that stimulated and excited dogs also bark. It is up to us to survey the surroundings and assess the reason. We need to educate ourselves about our dog's various barks so we can act appropriately.

## Whining and Whimpering

Almost from the time they are freshly made and feeding upon their mother's milk, our little puppies begin to make their first little fur-ball noises. Whimpering or whining to get their mothers attention for feeding or comfort is innate, and as a result, they know mom will come to them. They also use these two W's on us to gain our attention. Other reasons for whimpering or whining are from fear produced by loud noises such as thunderstorms or fireworks. I think most of us have experienced the 4th of July phenomenon where the entire dog population is barking excessively until the wee hours of the morning when the last fireworks are ignited, and the final "BOOM!" dies off.

## Growling

Growling means, you had better watch out. Be acutely aware of what this dog is doing or might do. Usually a dog that is growling is seriously irritated and preparing to be further aggressive. However, this is not always true, sometimes a dog will issue a growl requesting for petting to continue.

## Howling

Picture the dark silhouette of a howling dog with a full moon backdrop. A dog's howl is a distinct vocalization that most dogs use, and every wolf makes. Howling can mean loneliness, desire, warning, or excitement. A lonely howl is a dog looking for a response. Dogs also howl after a long hunt when they have tracked and cornered their prey. Some Scenthounds use a distinct sound named a bay.

### More in the NewDogJumpStartGuide

## ~ *Paws On – Paws Off* ~

# 26 Handle Me Gently

Teaching your Westie to be still, calm, and patient while he is being handled is a very important step in your relationship. When you master this one, it will make life easier for both of you when at home, and at the groomer or vet. Handling also helps when there is unwanted or accidental touching and especially when dealing with small children who love to handle dogs in all sorts of unusual and not so regular ways. This one will take patience and a few tricks to get started. Remember, that it is important to begin handling your new puppy immediately after you find each other and are living together.

The sooner your puppy accepts your touches and manipulations the easier life will be for the both of you. Handling is needed for grooming, bathing, lifting, and affection, medical procedures, inspecting for ticks, fleas, and caring for injuries.

Recognize that muzzles are not bad and do not hurt dogs. They can be an effective device and a great safety feature when your dog is learning to be handled. Easy cheese or peanut butter spread on the floor or on the refrigerator door can keep your puppy in place while he learns to be handled. If your puppy does not like to be handled, he will slowly learn to accept it.

*You must practice this with your puppy for at least one to three minutes each day so that he becomes comfortable with being touched.* All dogs are unique and therefore some will accept this easier and quicker than others will. Handling training will be a life-long process.

*With all of the following exercises, follow these steps*:

- Begin with short, non-intrusive gentle touching. *If your puppy is calm* and he is not trying to squirm away, use a word such as "good," "nice," or "yes," and give your pup a treat.

- If your puppy squirms, keep touching him but do not fight his movements, keeping your hand lightly on him while moving your hand with his squirms. Use your hand as though it were a suction cup and stuck to the place that you are touching. When he settles, treat him and remove your hand.

- Work from one second to ten seconds or more, gradually working your way up to touching for longer durations, such as 2,4,6,8 to 10 seconds.

- Do not go forward to another step until your puppy adapts, and enjoys the current step.

- *Do not* work these exercises more than a couple of minutes at a time. Overstimulation can cause your puppy stress. Continue slowly at your puppy's comfortable speed.

## Handling the Body

### Paws

It is a fact that most puppies do not like to have their paws touched. Proceed slowly with this exercise. The eventual goal is for your puppy to adore his paws being fondled. In the following exercises, any time your puppy does not squirm and try to get away, *click and treat* your pup. If he does squirm, stay with him using gentle contact, when your pup ceases wiggling, then *click and treat*, and release when he calms down. Each one of these steps will take a few days to complete and will require at least a dozen repetitions.

Confirm that you successfully complete each step and your puppy is at least tolerant of the contact before you go on to the next one.

- *Do each step with all four paws, and remember to pause a minute between paws, allowing your pup to regain his composure.*

- Pick up your puppy's paw and immediately click and treat. Repeat this five times and then continue forward by adding an additional one second each time you pick up his paw until ten seconds is reached.

Hold the paw for ten to twelve seconds with no struggling from your dog. Begin with two seconds then in different sessions work your way to twelve.

During holding the paw, begin adding the following.

- Hold the paw and move it around.

- Massage the paw.

- Pretend to trim the nails.

*Side Note:* Do not trim your dog's nails unless you are positively sure you know what you are doing. It is not easy and if you are not properly trained can cause extreme pain to your dog.

## The Collar

*Find a quiet, low distraction place to practice, grab treats, and put your puppy's collar on him.*

- While gently restrained, touch your dog's collar underneath his chin, and then release him right away simultaneously clicking and treating him. Do this about ten times or until your puppy seems comfortable and relaxed with the process.

- Grab and hold the collar where it is under his chin and hold it for about 2 seconds, C/T, and repeat. Increase the amount of time until you have achieved about ten seconds of holding and your puppy remains calm. Click and treat after each elapsed amount of time. By increasing the hold time by 2 seconds, gradually work your way up to ten seconds of holding. This may take several days and sessions.

- Hold the collar under his chin and now give it a little tug. If he accepts this and does not resist, click and treat, and repeat. If he squirms, keep a gentle hold on the collar until he calms down, and then C/T and release him. Repeat this step until he is content with the procedure.

Now, switch to the top of the collar and repeat the whole progression again. Remember slowly increase the time held and the intensity of the tug.

You can pull or tug, but *do not jerk* your puppy's neck or head because this can cause injury and interfere with your outcome objectives of the training exercise. You can practice touching the collar while you are treating during training other tricks. Gently hold the bottom or top of the collar when you are giving your dog a treat reward for successfully completing a commanded behavior.

## Mouth

- Gently touch your puppy's mouth, *click and treat*, and repeat ten times.

- Touch the side of your puppy's mouth and lift a lip to expose a tooth, *click and treat*, then release only after he stops resisting.

- Gently and slowly, lift the lip to expose more and more teeth on both sides of the mouth, and then open the mouth. Then release when he does not resist, *click and treat*. Be cautious with this one.

- Touch a tooth with a toothbrush, then work up to brushing your puppy's teeth for one to ten-seconds, and then later increase the time. Brushing your puppy's teeth is something you will be doing a few times weekly for the lifetime of your dog.

**Ears**

- Reach around the side of your puppy's head, and then briefly and gently touch his ear. Click and treat, repeat ten times.

- When your puppy is comfortable with this, continue and practice holding the ear for one-second. If he is calm, click and treat. If he squirms, stay with him until he is calm. When your puppy calms down, click and treat, then release the ear. Do this until ten seconds is completed with no wiggling.

- Maneuver your pup's ear and pretend that you are cleaning it. Do this gently and slowly so that your puppy learns to enjoy it. It will take a few days of practice until your puppy is calm enough for the real ear cleaning. If your puppy is already sensitive about his ears being touched, it will take longer. See ear cleaning in the Basic Care section.

Proceed slowly at your puppy's comfortable pace. There is no rush just the end goal of your pup enjoying being handled in all sorts of ways that are beneficial to him.

**Tail**

Many puppies are sensitive about having their tails handled, and rightly so. Think about if someone grabs you by the arm and you are not fully ready. That is similar to the reaction a puppy feels when grabbed, especially when their tails are handled.

- Start by briefly touching his tail. When moving to touch your puppy's tail move slowly and let your hand be seen moving towards his tail. This keeps your puppy from being startled. Repeat this ten times with clicking and treating, until you notice your puppy is comfortable with his tail being touched.

- Increase the duration of time you hold his tail until you achieve the ten-second mark.

- Tenderly and cautiously, pull the tail up, brush the tail, and then tenderly pull on it until your dog allows you to do this without reacting by jerking, wiggling, or whimpering.

- Your Dog needs to be comfortable being touched on paws, ears, tail, mouth, entire body, and this should be practiced daily.

## Children

You must prepare your poor puppy to deal with the strange, unwelcome touching that is often exacted on them by children. Alternatively, you could just put a sign around his neck that says; "You must be at least 16 to touch this puppy." However, it is very likely that your puppy will encounter children that are touchy, grabby, or pokey.

- Prepare your puppy for the strange touches that children may perpetrate by practicing while clicking and treating him for accepting these odd bits of contact such as ear tugs, tail tugs, and perhaps a little harder than usual head pats, kisses, and hugs. Keep in mind, as previously mentioned, puppies and kids are not a natural pairing, *but cheese and wine are*. Even a puppy that is *good with kids* can be pushed to a breaking point and then things can get ugly, and nobody wants that.

*Always supervise children around your dog. ALWAYS! – It is a dog ownership law.*

## Lifting Dogs

An emergency may arise that requires you to pick up your dog. As you do these maneuvers, move and proceed slowly and cautiously. First, briefly put your arms around your dog and then give him a click and treat if he stays still. Increase the time duration with successive repetitions. Your dog should be comfortable for ten to fifteen seconds with your arms around him. Next, slowly proceed lifting your dog off the ground just a few inches or centimeters, and then back down. Each time he does not wriggle, click and treat. Increase the time and the distance that you lift him from the ground and then move your dog from one place to another. Calculate the time it might take to lift and carry your dog from the house and place him into your vehicle. This is a good time goal to set for carrying your dog.

Eventually, by lifting your dog up and placing him on a table, you will be able to prepare your dog for trips to the groomer, open spaces, or the vet. If you own an extra-large dog, or dog that is too heavy for you to lift, solicit help for this training from family or a friend. *Gigantor* may take two to lift safely and properly, or use one of the methods below.

Once up on the table you can practice handling in ways a groomer or veterinarian might handle your dog. This is good preparation for a day at the dog spa or veterinary procedures.

**How to lift a dog**

To lift a large dog properly, always start by approaching the dog from the side. Place one of your hands upon the dog's rear end with the tail in the down position, unless it is a curly tailed spitz type dog that will not enjoy having its tail forced down. This protects the dog's tail from being forced painfully upwards should your arm slip.

You should be holding your dog directly underneath the dog's rear hips. Your other hand should be in the front of the dog around his front legs with your arm across his chest. Now your arms should be on your dog's chest and butt area. Then gently press your arms together as in a cradling position and lift using your legs. The human's body position should be that of having bent legs and crouching down so that the power in the legs is used to lift you and your dog upright. To prevent injury to yourself, keep your back as straight as possible.

Small dogs are simpler to lift and require much less effort, but still take great care not to inadvertently injure them. Place your hand in between the back and front legs underneath the dog's underbelly. Supporting the rear with your forearm, additionally placing a hand on the dog's chest is a good idea for safety in the event that your dog squirms when being lifted.

For extra-large or dogs that are too heavy for you to lift, purchase and utilize a ramp so that your dog can walk itself into your vehicle. This saves you and your dog from possible or inevitable injury. It is always best to use caution instead of risking a painful, costly, or permanent injury. Of course, you can also teach your dog to jump into the vehicle. Later when your dog becomes aged, you can then utilize the ramp.

Some large dogs can be taught to put their front paws up onto the vehicle floorboard or tailgate, thus allowing you to help push them from their buttocks and assist them jumping in your vehicle.

Never grab, pull, or lift a dog by its fore or rear legs. This can cause serious pain and injury to a dog.

**Brushing**

- Get your puppy's brush and lightly touch him with it all over his body. If he remains unmoving, give him a click and treat, then repeat. Repeat this until you can brush every part of his body without him moving.

Your puppy will become comfortable with all varieties of touching and handling if you work slowly, patiently, and with plenty of good treats. Handling training is a very important step in your dog's socialization.

## ~ *Paws On – Paws Off* ~

# 27 Basic Care for Westies

Oral maintenance, nail clipping, and other grooming will depend upon you and your dog's activities. We all know our dogs love to roll and run through all sorts of possible ugly messes, and put obscene things into their mouths, then afterward run up to lick us. Depending upon your dog's coat curl then some of the processes below will need evaluation.

Below is a list of the basic grooming care your dog requires. Most basic care can easily be done at home by you, but if you are unsure or uncomfortable about something, seek tutelage and in no time you will be clipping, trimming, and brushing like a professional.

It is vital that handling training begin at the onset of bringing your puppy home because this will aid in all grooming, training, socialization, and potential medical procedures. Early handling of your dog is crucial for grooming because it will allow you or the groomer to perform grooming while manipulating all of your dog's body parts with little to no resistance. Most owners should be able to learn and perform some or all of the grooming techniques themselves.

If you are grooming your dog up on a table or slippery surface, first place a non-slip cloth or mat over that area so that your dog doesn't slip or move during the grooming process. This will avoid potential injury from scissors or shears.

Westies have a double coat that is comprised of a soft undercoat and a stiffer outer coat. The rough outer coat readily sheds dirt and protects the undercoat. Westies do not shed a lot of hair but the hair they shed becomes caught in there coat, so regular thorough brushing of the under and outer coat is necessary. Stay on top of any tangles so that they do not turn into mats. The softer undercoat doesn't begin to grow in until Westies are around one year old but it can take up to five years.

Puppies should be brushed at least once a week and adults daily. This will keep their coat in top condition and minimize you struggling with tangles and mats. Trimming with scissors and clippers is necessary to keep their look and coat tidy. Show dogs must be hand stripped and this is often done by professionals. It is a time consuming process but necessary to achieve the perfect look of a show coat.

Westie grooming equipment are a good pair of clippers with different sized blades, thinning shears, a good slicker brush and some metal teeth combs with different spacing.

To achieve the Westie look you should be taught by a groomer or breeder proper use and technique of all the grooming equipment. Having someone teach you will save you a lot of trial and error time and make your equipment investment worthwhile.

Always be patient and move slowly when grooming your dog head and muzzle area, their eyes, ears, nose, and mouth are all sensitive areas that can incur harm. Before you decide to groom your Westie yourself, learn the proper way to use shears and scissors when trimming around the head, muzzle and body. Depending upon the style you choose some of the grooming equipment can vary.

*Bathing* - Regular but not frequent bathing is essential. Much depends upon your dog's coat. Natural coat oils are needed to keep your dog's coat and skin moisturized. Never bathe your dog too frequently and brushing before bathing is recommended. Depending upon what your dog has been into, Westies do not require monthly bathing. Bathe only when needed. Their coat along with regular brushing keeps them clean.

Contending with stained beards can be tiresome, but if it really bothers you, can try whitening it with some diluted hydrogen peroxide or other homegrown remedies such as adding apple cider vinegar diluted with water to your dog's regular drinking water. Try one teaspoon per quart of water. Wash your dog's beard 1-2 times weekly with a white vinegar and water solution, a 50-50 solution of lemon juice and table salt with an egg white beaten into the combination. Leave the mixture on until dry and then brush out. Always be careful to keep any of these whitening solutions away from your dog's eyes.

- Supplies – Dog specific shampoo, 3-4 towels, nonslip bathmat for inside the tub.

- Shampoo – Use a dog shampoo made specifically for sensitive skin. This helps avoid any type of potential skin allergy, eye discomfort, and furthering pre-existing skin conditions.

- Coax your dog into the tub and shut the door (just in case he is not in the mood, or decides to bolt outside while still wet). We have all experienced this.

- Use warm water, not hot. Hot water tends to irritate the skin and can cause your dog to itch and then scratch. Do not use cold water on your dog.

- Apply enough shampoo to create lather over the body, but take care not to use so much that rinsing is difficult and time consuming. Rub into lather, avoiding the eyes and ears.

- Bathe the head area last.

- Rinse repeatedly and thoroughly to avoid skin irritation.

- Thoroughly dry your dog by using a towel. If it is cold outside you will want to finish by using a low setting hair dryer. Additionally, a slicker brush can be used while drying, remembering to brush in the direction of the hair growth.

*Nail trimming* – For optimal foot health, your dog's nails should be kept short. There are special clippers that are needed for nail trimming that are designed to avoid injury. You can start trimming when your dog is a puppy, and you should have no problems. However, if your dog still runs for the hills or squirms like an eel at trimming time, then your local groomer or veterinarian can do this procedure.

Dog's nails are composed of a hard outer shell named the *horn* and a soft cuticle in the center known as the *quick*. The horn has no nerves and thus has no feeling. The quick is composed of blood vessels and nerves, and therefore needs to be avoided.

Black nails make the quick harder to identify. White nails allow the quick to be recognized by its pink coloring. Dogs that spend a lot of time walking and running on rough surfaces tend to have naturally shortened quicks. Furthermore, the quick grows with the nails, so diligent nail trimming will keep the quick receded.

- Identify where the quick is located in your dog's nails. The object will be to trim as close (2mm) to the quick as possible without nipping the quick and causing your dog pain and possibly bleeding.

- To identify the quick in black nails, begin cutting small pieces from the end of the nail and examine underneath the nail. When you see a uniform gray oval appear at the top of the cut surface, then stop further cutting. Behind the gray is where the quick is located, if you see pink then you have passed the gray and arrived at the quick. If you have done this, your dog is probably experiencing some discomfort. *The goal is to stop cutting when you see the gray.*

-File the cut end to smooth the surface.

- If you accidentally cut into the quick, apply styptic powder. If not available, cornstarch or flour can be substituted.

- If your dog challenges your cutting, be diligent and proceed without verbal or physical abuse, and reward after successful trimming is completed. If you encounter the occasional challenge, your diligence should curtail the objection. If you manage never to cut into your dog's quick, this helps prevent any negative associations with the process, but some dogs simply do not enjoy the handling of their paws or nail trimming.

*Ear cleaning* – You should clean your dog's ears at least once a month, but be sure to inspect them every few days for bugs such as mites and ticks. Also, look for any odd discharge, which can be an indication of infection, requiring a visit to the vet. Remember to clean the outer ear only, by using a damp cloth or a cotton swab doused with mineral oil.

*Eye cleaning* –

Whenever you are grooming your dog, check their eyes for any signs of damage or irritation. Other dog signals for eye irritation are if your dog is squinting, scratching, or pawing at their eyes. You should contact your veterinarian if you notice that the eyes are cloudy, red, or have a yellow or green discharge.

Use a moist cotton ball to clean any discharge from the eye. Avoid putting anything irritating around, or into your dog's eyes.

*Brushing teeth* - Pick up a specially designed canine tooth brush and cleaning paste. Clean your dog's teeth as frequently as daily. Try to brush your dog's teeth a few times a week at a minimum. If your dog wants no part of having his or her teeth brushed, try rubbing his teeth and gums with your finger. After he is comfortable with this, you can now put some paste on your finger, allowing him to smell and lick it, then repeat rubbing his teeth and gums with your finger. Now that he is comfortable with your finger, repeat with the brush. In addition, it is important to keep plenty of chews around to promote the oral health of your pooch. When your dog is 2-3 years old, he or she may need their first professional teeth cleaning.

*Anal sacs* - These sacs are located on each side of a dog's anus. If you notice your dog scooting his rear, or frequently licking and biting at his anus, the anal sacs may be impacted. When you notice this, it is time to release some fluid from them using a controlled method. If you are not comfortable doing this, you can ask your veterinarian how to diagnose and treat this issue.

Both the male and female dogs have anal glands and they are found directly beneath the skin that surrounds the anal muscles. The other name for them is scent glands. These glands tell other dogs the mood of a dog, health, and gender, which is why so much but sniffing goes on between dogs.

To release the fluid when they are enlarged it is good practice to place your Westie inside a bathtub. The fluid is pungent and brownish in color so tub protects anything that might come into contact.

Place a finger on each side of the sac, then apply pressure upwards and inwards towards the rectum and this is when you should see the fluid come out. If for some reason fluid does not come out, then seek assistance because if they are enlarged, they need to be emptied.

## *~ Paws On – Paws Off ~*

# 28 Dog Nutrition

As for nutrition, humans study it, practice it, complain about it, but usually give into the science and common sense of it. Like humans, dogs have their own nutrition needs and charts to follow, and are subject to different theories and scientific studies, as well.

Like humans, dogs have their own nutrition needs and charts to follow and are subject to different theories and scientific studies as well.

In the beginning, there were wild packs of canines everywhere and they ate anything that they could get their paws on. Similar to human survival, dogs depended upon meat from kills, grasses, berries, and other edibles that nature provided. What is the great news? Many millennia later nature is still providing all that we need.

In history, the Romans wrote about feeding their dogs barley bread soaked in milk along with the bones of sheep. The wealthy Europeans of the 1800's would feed their dogs better food than most humans had to eat. Meat from horses and other dead animals was often rounded up from the streets to recycle as dog food for the rich estates on the outskirts of cities.

Royalty is legendary for pampering their dogs with all sorts of delicacies from around the world. Meanwhile, the poor and their dogs had to fend for themselves or starve. Being fed table scraps from a pauper's diet was not sufficient to keep a dog healthy, and the humans themselves often had their own nutrition problems. To keep from starving dogs would hunt rats, rabbits, mice and any other rodent or insect type creature that they could sink their teeth into. This practice continues today around the globe.

In the mid to late 1800's a middle class blossomed out of the industrial revolution. This new class with its burgeoning wealth had extra money to spend and started taking on dogs as house pets. Unwittingly they created an enterprise out of feeding the suddenly abundant household pets.

Noting that the sailor's biscuits kept well for long periods, James Spratt began selling his own recipe of hard biscuits for dogs in London, and shortly thereafter, he took his new product to New York City. It is believed that he single-handedly started the American dog food business. This places the dog food and kibble industry at just over 150 years old, and now is an annual multi-billion dollar business.

All the while we know that any farm, feral or other dog that can kill something and eat it will do just that. Nothing has changed throughout the centuries. Raw meat does not kill dogs, so it is safe to say that raw food diets will not either. If you are a bit tentative about the idea of raw foods, cooking the meats you serve your dog is a viable option.

**Feeding Your Puppy and Adult Dog**

To check if your puppy is having its proper dietary needs met, check to make sure that your puppy is active, alert, and is showing good bone and muscle development. To understand the correct portion to feed your dog, ask the breeder to show you the portion that they feed their puppies.

Then observe whether your puppy is quickly devouring their food and then acting as though he wants and needs more. If so, then increase the portion a little until you find the correct serving. If your puppy is eating quickly, then begins to nibble, and finally leaves foods in the bowl, then you are over-feeding him.

As you adjust the food portion to less or more; observe whether your puppy is gaining or losing weight so that you can find the proper portion of food to serve during feeding times. Very active puppies tend to burn lots of energy and this is one reason that a puppy might need a little extra food in their bowl. The suggested portions are on the food containers, but this world is not a one-size-fits-all place. Observation and note keeping is needed to determine the correct portions for you individual dog.

Many breeders and trainers state that puppies should not leave their mothers until they are at least eight weeks old. This allows their mother's milk to boost their immunity by supporting antibodies and nutrition that are needed to become a healthy dog. Around three to four weeks old puppies should begin eating some solid food in conjunction with their mother's milk. This helps their digestion process begin to adjust to solid foods making the transition from mother's milk to their new home and foods easier.

Puppies are going to eat four times a day up until about eight weeks. At eight weeks, they can still be fed four times a day, or you can reduce to three times. Split the recommend daily feeding portion into thirds. Puppies' nutritional requirements differ from adult dogs so select a puppy food that has the appropriate balance of nutrients that puppies require. Puppy food should continue to support healthy growth, digestion, and the immune system. Supplying your growing puppy with the correct amount of calories, protein, and calcium is part of a well-balanced diet.

When choosing your puppy's feeding times, choose the times that you know will be the best for you to feed your puppy. Feeding on a regular schedule is one part of over-all *consistency* that you are establishing for your puppy to know that as the alpha you are reliably satisfying their needs. After setting the feeding schedule, remain as close to those times as possible. For example, 7 am, around noon, and again at 5pm. An earlier dinnertime helps your puppy to digest then eliminate before their bedtime.

During the three to six month puppy stage, teething can alter your puppies eating habits. Some pups may not feel like eating due to pain, so it is your responsibility to remain diligent in your job to provide them all of their nutritional requirements and confirm that they are eating.

*Hint*: Soaking their dry food in water for 10-15 minutes before feeding will soften it and make it easier for your puppy to eat. This avoids suddenly introducing new different softer foods to your puppy and avoids the unknown consequences.

At six months to a year old, your puppy still requires high quality nutritionally charged foods. Consult your breeder or veterinarian about the right time to switch to an adult food. Variance exists because some breeds have a longer puppyhood than others do.

When you switch to an adult food, continue to choose the highest quality food that has a specified meat, and not only by-products. Avoid unnecessary artificial additives. In many cases, higher quality foods that you feed your dog allow you to serve smaller portions because more of the food is being used by your dog and not just flowing through. Fillers are often not digested and this requires feeding your dog larger portions.

Additionally, follow the alpha guideline that states that *humans always eat first*. This means that the humans finish their meal entirely and clear the table before feeding their dogs, or feed your dog a couple of hours before you and your family eat. This establishes and continues the precedence that all humans are above the dog in the pecking order.

**Help Identifying Dog Food Quality**

• The first ingredient, or at a minimum, the second should specify *meat* or *meat meal*, NOT by-product.

• *"What is a by-product?"* Unless specified on the label, a by-product can be left over parts from animals and contain parts of hooves, feet, skin, eyes, or other animal body parts.

• Beware of ingredients that use wording such as *animal* and *meat* instead of a specific word such as beef or chicken.

• "Meal" when listed in ingredients is something that has been weighed after the water was taken out, an example would be *chicken meal*. This means it has been cooked with a great amount of water reduction occurring in the process, and thus it is providing more actual meat and protein per weight volume.

As an example, if the dog food package only states "beef" in the ingredients, it refers to the pre-cooking weight. This means that after cooking, less meat will be present in the food.

• A label that states "beef" first then "corn meal" secondly, is stating that the food probably contains a lot more corn than beef. Corn is not easily digested nor does it offer much in the way of nutrients that are vital to a dog's health. Furthermore, it has been linked to other health issues, and dogs are not designed to eat corn and grains in high doses. Try your best to avoid corn, wheat, and soy in your dog's food. The higher quality more expensive foods are often worth the cost to advance your dog's health.

• If you decide to change dog food formulas or brands, a gradual change over is recommended, especially if your dog has a sensitive stomach. This is done by mixing some of the old with the new, and then throughout the week gradually increasing the amount of new.

**An example schedule of changing dog foods**

Day 1-2 Mix ¼ new with ¾ old foods

Day 2-4 Mix ½ new with ½ old

Day 5-6 Mix ¾ new with ¼ old

Day 7 100% of the new dog food

**The Switch - Moving From Puppy to Adult Food**

When your puppy is ready to make the switch from puppy to adult dog food, you can follow the same procedure above, or shorten it to a four to five day switch over. During the switch, be observant of your dog's stools and health.

If your dog appears not to handle the new food formula then your options are to change the current meat to a different meat, or try a different formula or brand. Avoid returning to the original puppy food. If you have any concerns or questions, consult your veterinarian or breeder.

# Raw Foods

Let us first remember that our dogs, pals, best friends, comedy actors, were meant to eat real foods such as meat. Their DNA does not only dictate them to eat dry cereals that were concocted by humans in white lab coats. These cereals based and meat-by products ingredients may have been keeping our pets alive, but in many cases not thriving at optimum levels.

There are many arguments for the benefits of real and raw foods. Sure it is more work, but isn't their health worth it? It is normal, not abnormal to be feeding your dog, a living food diet; it is believed that it will greatly boost their immune system and over-all health. A raw food diet is based off pre-dog food diets and is a return to their wild hunting and foraging days and pre-manmade biscuit foods.

There are different types of raw food diets. There are raw meats that you can prepare at home by freeze-drying or freezing that can then be easily thawed to feed your dog, commercially pre-packaged frozen raw foods, or offering up an entire whole animal. All of these diets take research and careful attention so that you are offering your dog all that they need, and something that their bodies can easily tolerate. Correct preparation of raw foods diets needs to be understood, for example, it is suggested that vegetables are cut into very small pieces or even pureed.

Raw food diets amount to foods that are not cooked or sent through a processing plant. With some research, you can make a decision on what you think is the best type of diet for your dog. For your dog's health and for their optimal benefits it is worth the efforts of your research time to read up on a raw foods diet, a mix of kibble and raw foods, or raw and cooked foods. *All foods,* dry, wet, or raw contain a risk, as they can all contain contaminants and parasites.

Known benefits are fewer preservatives, chemicals, hormones, steroids, and the addition of fruits and vegetables into their diet. Physically your dog can have firmer stools, reduced allergies, improved digestion, healthier coat and skin, and over-all improved health.

Some of the negative attributes are the lack of convenience versus kibble and potential bacterial contamination. However, dogs are at a lowered risk for salmonella and E. coli than humans are. A dog's digestive system is more acidic and less prone to such diseases; the greater risk is to the preparer. Many experts state that the overall risk of a *properly prepared* raw food diet is minimal.

There is a process named HPP (High Pressure Pasteurization) which most pre-prepared raw food brands utilize in their processing that does not use heat but eliminates harmful bacteria without killing off good bacteria.

**Rules of thumb to follow for a raw food diet**

1. Before switching, make sure that your dog has a healthy gastro-intestinal track.

2. Be smart, and do not leave un-refrigerated meats for prolonged periods.

3. To be safe, simply follow human protocol for food safety. Toss out the smelly, slimy, or the meat and other food items that just do not seem fit for consumption.

4. Keep it balanced. Correct amount of vitamins and minerals, fiber, antioxidants, and fatty acids. Note any medical issues your dog has, and possible diet correlations.

5. If switching from bag or can, a gradual switch over between foods is recommended to allow their GI track to adjust. Use new foods as a treat, and then watch stools to see how your dog is adjusting.

6. Take note of the size and type of bones you throw to your dog. Not all dogs do well with real raw bones because slivers, splinters, and small parts can become lodged in their digestive tracks. Always provide the freshest bones possible to dogs. *Never give dogs cooked bones.*

7. Freezing meats for three days, similar to sushi protocol, can help kill unwanted pathogens or parasites.

8. Remember to be vigilant, and take note of your observations about what is working and not working with your dog's food changes. If your dog has a health issue, your veterinarian will thank you for your detailed note taking.

9. Like us humans, most dogs do well with a variety of foods. There is no one-size-fits-all diet.

10. Before switching over, please read about raw foods diets and their preparation and follow all veterinary guidelines.

"BARF®" is an acronym that means Biologically Appropriate Raw Food. It is a complete and carefully balanced blend of raw meat, fruits, vegetables and bone. The formula mimics what nature designed for our pet's to thrive on in the wild. The result is a pet free of allergies, digestive problems, and full of life!

In summary, the first line of defense against disease is feeding your dog a proper diet which includes feeding them *premium* dry food, canned food, Raw food or (BARF diet), home cooked food or any combination of these.

# Vitamins – Nutrients - Minerals

According to nutritional scientists and veterinarian health professionals, your dog needs twenty Amino Acids, ten of which are essential. At least thirty-six nutrients and a couple of extra may be needed to combat certain afflictions. Your dog's health depends upon the intake of the following nutrients. Read labels and literature to take stock of the foods you provide your canine.

It may take time to understand what kind of diet your dog will thrive. Do your best to include in your dog's daily diet, all thirty-six nutrients mentioned here. All of which can come from fruits, veggies, kibble, raw foods, and yes, even good table scraps. You will soon discover that your dog has preferred foods.

For your dog to maintain optimum health, he needs a daily basis of a GI track healthy, well-rounded diet with a good balance of exercise, rest, socializing, care, and love.

**36 Nutrients for dogs:**

1. 10 essential Amino Acids – Arginine, Histidine, Isoleucine, Leucine, Lysine, Methionine, additionally Phenylalanine, Threonine, Tryptophan, and Valine.

2. 11 vitamins – A, D, E, B1, B2, B3, B5, B6, B12, Folic Acid, and Choline.

3. 12 minerals – Calcium, Phosphorus, Potassium, Sodium, Chloride, Iron, Magnesium, Copper, Manganese, Zinc, Iodine, and Selenium.

4. Fat – Linoleic Acid

5. Omega 6 Fatty Acid

6. Protein

# Human Foods for Dogs

Many human foods are safe for dogs. In reality, human and dog foods were similar for most of our coexistence. Well, maybe we wouldn't eat some of the vermin they eat, but if we were hungry enough we could.

Whether you have your dog on a raw food diet, a partial raw food diet, or manufactured dog foods, you can still treat with some human foods. Even a top quality dog food may be lacking in some nutrients your dog may need. In addition, a tasty safe human food, such as an apple can be used as a treat in training. Below is a short list of some safe human foods that you may feed your dog. Remember to proceed in moderation to see how your dog's digestive system reacts and adjusts to each different food. Always keep plenty of clean fresh drinking water available for your dog.

## Short List of SAFE Human Foods for Dogs

### Oatmeal

Oatmeal is a fantastic alternative human food source of grain for dogs that are allergic to wheat. Oatmeal's fiber can also be beneficial to more mature dogs. A general set of rules can be followed when feeding your dog oatmeal. Limit the serving sizes, and amount of serving times per week, be sure to serve the oatmeal fully cooked, and finally never add any sugar or additional flavoring.

### Apples

REMOVE the seeds. Apples are an excellent human food safe for dogs to crunch on. My dog loves to munch on apples. Apples offer small amounts of both vitamin C and Vitamin A. They are a good source of fiber for a dog of any age. Caution! Do not let your dog eat the seeds of the apple OR the core as they are known to contain minute amounts of cyanide. A few will not be detrimental, so do not freak out if it happens. Just be cautious and avoid the core and seeds when treating.

### Brewer's Yeast

This powder has a tangy taste that dogs will clamber to get. The yeast is rich in B vitamins, which are great for the dog's skin, nails, ears, and coat.

Do not confuse this with 'baking yeast,' which can make your dog ill if eaten. All you need to do is add a couple of sprinkles of brewer's yeast on your dog's food to spice it up. Most dogs really enjoy this stuff.

Brewer's yeast is made from a one-celled fungus called Saccharomyces cerevisiae and is used to make beer. Brewer's yeast is a rich source of minerals, particularly chromium, which is an essential trace mineral that helps the body maintain normal blood sugar levels, selenium, protein, and the B-complex vitamins. Brewer's yeast has been used for years as a nutritional supplement.

## Eggs

Does your dog need a protein boost? Eggs are a super supplemental food because they contain ample amounts of protein; selenium, riboflavin, and they are also easily digested by your dog. Cook eggs before serving them to your best friend, because the cooking process makes more protein available, and it make them more digestible. Eggs are good for energy, strength, and great for training as well.

## Green Beans

A lean dog is a happier, more energetic dog. Feeding your dog, cooked green beans is a good source of manganese, and the vitamins C and K, additionally is they are considered a good source of fiber. If you have a lazier dog, living *"A Dog's Life,"* then it is good to be proactive with your dog's weight. Add a steady stream of fresh green beans in your dog's diet for all the right reasons. Avoid salt.

## Sweet Potatoes

Vitamin C, B-6, manganese, beta-carotene, and fiber can be found in sweet potatoes. Slice them up and dehydrate and you have just found a great new healthy source for treating your dog. Next time you are out shopping for potatoes, pick up sweet potatoes, and see if your best little buddy takes to them. My bet is that your dog will love them.

## Pumpkins

Pumpkins are a fantastic source of vitamin A, fiber, and beta-carotene. Trend towards a healthy diet with plenty of fiber and all the essential vitamins and proteins your dog needs. Pumpkin is one way to help you mix it up a bit. Feed it dried or moist, separate as a treat, or with his favorite foods. Pumpkin can be a fantastic, fun, and natural alternative food for dogs.

## Salmon

A great source of omega 3 fatty acids, salmon is an excellent food that can support your dog's immune system, as well as his skin, coat, and overall health. Some dog owners notice when adding salmon to their dog's diet that it increases resistance to allergies. Be sure to cook the salmon before serving it. You can use salmon oil too. For treats, added flavoring to a meal, or as a complete meal, salmon is a fantastic source of natural, real food that is safe for dogs.

## Flax Seed

Grounded or in oil form, flax seed is a nourishing source of omega 3 fatty acids. Omega 3 fatty acids are essential in helping your dog maintain good skin and a shiny healthy coat. Note; you will want to serve the flax seed directly after grinding it because this type of fatty acid can turn sour soon after. Flax seed is also a wonderful source of fiber your dog or puppy needs.

## Yogurt

Always a great source for your dog's calcium and protein, yogurt is another one of our top ten human foods safe for dogs. Pick a fat free yogurt with no added sweeteners, or artificial sugar, color, or flavoring.

## Melons

Additionally, watermelons, cantaloupes, honeydews are good for your dog. Without prior research, avoid any exotic melons or fruits.

## Peanut butter

Yep, a big spoon full and it will keep him occupied for a while.

## Berries (fresh & frozen)

Blueberries, blackberries, strawberries, huckleberries or raspberries provide an easy and tasty snack.

## Cooked chicken

Chicken sliced up is a favorite yummy snack for your canine to enjoy in addition, or in place of his regular meal.

## Beef and Beef Jerky & Cooked Meats

Jerky is a great high-value treating item for training, and beef is can be a healthy addition to your dog's diet. Cooked meats are a good addition or substitution for manufactured dog foods.

## Cheese

Sliced or cubed pieces are great for training or in the place of food. A tablespoon of cottage cheese on top of your dog's food will certainly be a healthy hit. Try using string cheese as a training treat.

## Bananas

All fruits have phytonutrients, and other required nutrients that are essential to your canine's health.

## Carrots

Crunchy veggies are good for the teeth. Carrots are full of fiber and vitamin A.

## UNSAFE Human Foods

Below is a list of harmful foods for dogs. This is not a complete list, but a common list of foods known to be harmful to our canine friends. If you are unsure of a food that you wish to add to your dog's diet, please consult a veterinarian or expert on dog nutrition.

**Onions:** Both onions and garlic contain the toxic ingredient thiosulphate. However, onions are more dangerous than garlic because of this toxin. Many dog biscuits contain *trace* amounts of garlic, and because of this small amount, there is no threat to the health of your dog. This poison can be toxic in one large dose, or with repeated consumption that builds to the toxic level in the dog's blood.

**Chocolate:** Contains theobromine, a compound that is a cardiac stimulant and a diuretic. This can be fatal to dogs.

**Grapes:** Contains an unknown toxin that can affect kidney, and in large enough amounts can cause acute kidney failure.

**Raisins:** (Same as above)

**Most Fruit Pits and Seeds:** Contains cyanogenic glycosides, which if consumed can cause cyanide poisoning. The fruits by themselves are okay to consume.

**Macadamia Nuts:** Contains an unknown toxin that can be fatal to dogs.

**Most Bones:** Should not be given (especially chicken bones) because they can splinter and cause a laceration of the digestive system or pose a choking hazard because of the possibility for them to become lodged in your pet's throat.

**Potato Peelings and Green Potatoes:** Contains oxalates, which can affect the digestive, nervous, and urinary systems.

**Rhubarb leaves:** Contains high amount of oxalates.

**Broccoli:** Broccoli should be avoided, though it is only dangerous in large amounts.

**Green parts of tomatoes:** Contains oxalates, which can affect the digestive, nervous, and urinary systems.

**Yeast dough:** Can produce gas and swell in your pet's stomach and intestines, possibly leading to a rupture of the digestive system.

**Coffee and tea:** (due to the caffeine)

**Alcoholic Beverages:** Alcohol is very toxic to dogs and can lead to coma or even death.

**Human Vitamins**: Vitamins containing iron are especially dangerous. These vitamins can cause damage to the lining of the digestive system, the kidneys, and liver.

**Moldy or spoiled foods:** There are many possible harmful outcomes from spoiled foods.

**Persimmons:** These can cause intestinal blockage.

**Raw Eggs:** Potential for salmonella.

**Salt:** In large doses can cause an electrolyte imbalance.

**Mushrooms**: Can cause liver and kidney damage.

**Avocados:** Avocado leaves; fruit, seeds, and bark contain a toxin known as persin. The Guatemalan variety that is commonly found in stores appears to be the most problematic. Avocados are known to cause respiratory distress in other animals, but causes less harmful problems in dogs. It is best to avoid feeding them to your dog.

**Xylitol:** This artificial sweetener is not healthy for dogs.

## ~ *Paws On – Paws Off* ~

Please take the time to REVIEW this West Highland Terrier training guide and tell others about the positive information inside.

REVIEW NOW by going to the Amazon Page below and posting your *positive review*.

## https://www.amazon.com/dp/B00I5XB49K

Thank you

Paul

# 29  That's All Folks

Believe me, this is not everything that there is to know about dogs. Training your West Highland Terrier is a lifelong endeavor. There are a myriad of other methods, tricks, tools, and things to teach and learn with your dog. You are never finished, but this is half of the fun of having a dog, as he or she is a constant work in progress. Your dog is living art.

If your training experience is anything similar to mine, there were days and times when you thought your dog would never catch on, or seemed interested in participating and learning. I hope that you were able to work through the difficult times and the result is that you and your dog now understand one another at a high level, and that you are in command of your dog.

Owning and befriending our dogs is a lifetime adventurous commitment that is worthwhile and rewarding on every level. It seems as though many times Axel knows what I am thinking and acts or reacts accordingly, but he and I are together more than most of my family members. Through the good and bad times, he always makes me smile, sometimes when he is being the orneriest I smile the biggest. He is such a foolhardy, loveable, intelligent, and clownish dog, how could anyone be sad around him.

Remember, it is important to learn to think like your dog. Patience with your dog, as well as with yourself is vital. If you do this right, you will have a relationship and a bond that will last for years. The companionship of a dog can bring joy and friendship like none other. Keep this book handy and reference it often. In addition, look for other resources, such as training books, and utilizing like-minded experienced friends with dogs that can share their successes and failures. Never stop broadening your training skills. Your efforts will serve to keep you and your West Highland Terrier happy and healthy for a long, long time.

Thanks for reading! I hope that you enjoyed this as much as I have enjoyed writing it. If this training guide informed how to train your dog, please review this guide and tell others about the positive information in this guide. I am always striving to improve both my writing and training skills. I look forward to reading your comments.

## ~ *Paws On – Paws Off* ~

# DON'T THiNK - BE ALPHA DOG

I wrote this book to inform and instruct dog owners of the fundamentals for establishing and maintaining the *alpha* position within the household hierarchy. Inside the book you will learn how to live, lead, train, and love your dog in a ***non-physical alpha dog way***. Leading from the *alpha* position makes everything dog related *easier*. All dogs need to know where they are positioned within the family (pack), and to understand, and

 trust that their *alpha* will provide food, shelter, guidance, and affection towards them. Then life becomes *easier* for you and your dog.

Whether or not you have read one of my "Think Like a dog…" breed specific training books, I am confident that this guide will assist you while you train your dog companion. With these *alpha* fundamentals, your dog will obey your commands in critical situations, and follow your lead into a safer and happier life.

Remember, having an obedient dog keeps other animals and humans safe.

A dog that respects his *alpha* leader is easier to control, teach, and trust. He is more likely to obey your commands and respect your rules. Be the *alpha* now.

### "Alpha Dog Secrets" by Paul Allen Pearce
### LEARN MORE
### amazon.com/dp/B00ICGQO40

*Hey...Did I miss something?*

## STUMPED?

## Got a Question about Your West Highland Terrier?

*Ask an Expert Now!*

**Facebook**

**facebook.com/newdogtimes**

**NewDogTimes.com**

*It's where the* **West Highland Terrier Secrets** *have been hidden -since their Ancestral Wolf Packs were forced to collide with Man...*

### Wait Until You Learn This

# 31  2 BONUS TRICKS


Teaching the "Touch" & How to Learn Names


**The Following Tricks are Excerpted from**

**"49 ½ Dog Tricks"**

**By Paul Allen Pearce**

**Available Soon**

## Introduction

*Did you ever want to amaze and entertain your friends and family with the type of dog that can, will, and wants to do anything at any time, a show-off dog? You know that dog that understands vocal and body signals, reacts when commanded, and is a great companion in life. The tricks inside this book are the kind of fun and useful tricks that can give you that kind of dog when together you master them. After training these tricks included inside this book, you and your dog can have a joyful and fruitful life together as friends and partners in showmanship.*

# Trick #10 Teaching "Touch"

*Touch has an easy rating and requires no knowledge of other tricks, but your dog should know its name, and sit is helpful. The supplies needed are a wooden dowel to be used as a touch stick, your clicker, and some treats.*

*Touch* training teaches your dog to touch, and in this lesson to touch the end of a stick. It can be any type of wooden dowel, cut broom handle, or similar that is around three feet (1 meter) in length. During training, add a plastic cap, rubber ball, or good ole duct tape to the end so that there are no sharp edges that can harm your dog. A good sanding will also cure the problem of rough or sharp edges.

Teaching "touch" using the *touch stick* will enable you to train other tricks. You will discover that the *touch stick* is useful in training, so take care that you correctly train your dog the *touch* command. Touch is used later to teach Learn Names, Ring Bell, Jump Over People, Spin, Jump, and more.

**1.** Begin training in a quiet place with few distractions, and bring plenty of treats.

**2.** Start with your dog in the sitting position or standing near you and giving his attention towards you. Hold your stick away from your body. Keep holding it while doing nothing else but holding the stick steady at a level that your dog can easily touch it with his nose.

**3.** Luckily, dog's natural curiosity will get the best of them and your dog should touch the stick. When your dog touches it with his nose or mouth, *click and treat*. Be sure to click immediately when your dog touches the end of the stick. Sometimes it is just a sniff, but those count for beginning to shape the command and require a C/T to let your dog understand what behavior you are seeking.

If your dog is not interested then you will need to do the touching for him. Do this by gently touching your dog's nose while simultaneously clicking and then treating. Keep doing this until your dog is regularly touching the stick when you hold it out.

**4.** The next time your dog touches the stick C/T while simultaneously saying the command, "touch." Remember timing is important in all tricks. Your dog needs to know the exact action that is the correct action, which he is being rewarded for performing. Repeat this a dozen times. Continue over multiple sessions until your dog upon the command of "touch," is easily touching the end of the touch stick. Feel free to add some "good dog" praises.

**Hands On**

Teaching Jake this trick was an interesting outing. When I first held out the stick, Jake swiped it away with his paw. After a couple of more times, he finally smelled the end with his nose and I quickly clicked and treated. He responded to that, and after reinforcing that with several more *click and treats*, he started quickly touching the end of the stick.

After using the *touch* command a dozen times, he realized a treat came after he touched the end of the stick, and moving forward through a few training sessions, he started touching it each time I issued my "touch" command. I kept practicing and after a couple of more sessions, I locked it in with Jake. I was then able to use the "touch" command and touch stick to train other tricks.

If your dog is coming in hard to touch the stick, you can add some foam to the end of the stick to cushion his *super-nose*.

**Troubleshooting**

*What if my dog is touching the middle of the stick, or not touching the stick at all?*

I mentioned that Jake took a few swipes at the end of the stick before touching it. Each time he did this, I ignored this behavior even though he looked at me expecting a reward. He could smell the treats in my hand, but I did not click and reward the wrong action. Finally, as I held the stick out close to his snout, he smelled it with his nose and I quickly clicked and treated.

Do not reward until your dog is touching *only* the end of the stick. This allows you to use the touch command in training other tricks. If your dog will not touch it try gently touching the end of the stick to his nose and C/T, but quickly move away from that and let your dog begin to do the touching on his own.

# Health Insurance
## for my Dog?
### *Really?* Why?

*Because Paying Cash Makes No "Cents" or Does It?*

*Shocking Statistics!* **Discover the Truth!**

Type Into Your Browser

http://nobrainerdogtrainer.com/insurance-for-dogs/

Please take the time to REVIEW this West Highland Terrier training guide and tell others about the positive information inside.

REVIEW NOW by going to the Amazon Page below and posting your *positive review*.

## https://www.amazon.com/dp/B00I5XB49K

Thank you

Paul

# Trick #15 - Learn Names

*Learning names has an intermediate to difficult rating and requires knowledge of the touch command. The supplies needed are a toy, treats, and your clicker.*

Dog owners have known for years that dogs are smarter than many people give them credit. They are capable of learning the names of many different objects such as their toys, people, and places such as rooms. Using the steps in this exercise your dog can learn the names of all your family members, his personal items such as his crate, collar, and leash. Beyond those items, your dog can learn the names of different rooms, which enable you to use the "go" command to have your dog, go to a specific room. Dogs have been known to learn hundreds and even upwards to a thousand words. Furthermore, once your dog learns the name of something, he or she can find it, take it, and bring it to you.

Not all dogs are capable of learning the same number of words and some will learn and retain better than others, so do not get frustrated if it takes some time for your dog to recognize and remember what object, place, or person goes with the name you are speaking. Select a toy that you may already refer to by name. Chances are that you already often speak the names of dog-associated items when speaking to your dog and he recognizes that word. Be consistent in your name references to your dog's toys such as Frisbee™, tug, ball, rope, and squeaky.

**1.** To begin, find a low distraction area, treats at the ready, and one of your dog's favorite toys. I will use *tug* in this example.

**2.** Start by using *touch* and have your dog touch your empty hand, when he does, *click and treat* your dog. Repeat this five times.

**3.** Next, grab your dog's toy into your hand, say, "touch," and if he touches the tug and not your hand, C/T your dog.

**4.** Repeat number three, but this time, add the toy name, say, "touch tug." When your dog touches the *tug*, and nothing else, C/T at that exact moment he does this. Repeat this 6-10 times.

**5.** After a break, practice steps 1-4 over a few sessions, and a day or two.

**6.** In the next phase warm up with numbers 1-4, then hold the tug out away from you and say "touch tug," when he does C/T. Repeat this 6-10 times. Then extend the tug at full arm lengths from you and repeat 6-10 times. Practice this over a couple of sessions. Take note of your dog's progress and when he is ready, proceed to number seven.

**7.** Now, place the tug onto the floor but keep your hand on it, and say, "touch tug," when he does, C/T. Repeat 6-10 times.

**8.** Now, place it on the floor without your hand upon it, and say, "touch tug," and when he does, treat a barnbuster sized treat serving. Feel free to throw in some verbal good boy/girls. If your dog is not moving to it, be patient, silent, and still, and see if he can figure it out on his own. Remember that your dog wants his treat.

**9.** Moving forward with the same toy, place it around the room in different areas, increasingly further from you. Place it on top of a small stool, on the ground, and or low-lying shelves and have your dog "touch tug." Practice this over a few days and when your dog is regularly responding move onto number ten and a new toy.

**10.** Move onto another toy. Use a toy such as Frisbee™ that when said sounds much different when the word is spoken than the previous toy name. Repeat the steps 4-9 with this next toy.

**11.** Time to test if your dog can tell the difference. Sit down on the couch or floor and place both the Frisbee™ and the tug behind you. Take out the Frisbee and practice five touches, C/T each time your dog correctly touches upon command. Next, do the same with the tug.

**12.** Now, hold one toy in each hand and say, "touch Frisbee™" and see if your dog touches the correct toy. If your dog touches the Frisbee™, C/T, and then give a barnbuster sized reward. If your dog begins to move towards the Frisbee™, but you observe that he is unsure of himself, C/T for moving in the correct direction. If your dog goes to the tug or does nothing, remain neutral offering no C/T or verbal reward.

Keep working on this and practicing until your dog regularly goes to the correct toy that you command to be touched. Then following the same process continue adding toys. When you get to three, then four, toys/objects you can lay out all four in front of you and command "touch (object name)" and see if your dog can choose and recognize the correct toy/object.

**13.** Practice the "touch tug, ball, Frisbee, chew" by placing the objects in different parts of the room and have him identify each correctly. Practice this often to keep the names fresh in your dog's mind.

**14.** Teaching names of people is done a little differently, because for obvious reasons you cannot hold them in your hand, if they are willing, you could however have them sit on the floor. Trick #8 "Train Your Dog to Go To a Place" will teach you how to use the training stick to help train the names of rooms and things such as crate, bed, and mat. You can use the training stick to introduce the person.

**Alternative to #14 -** Teaching a person's name to your dog can be taught like this.

**1.** Hold onto your dog's collar and have a family member show your dog a treat. Have the person walk into the other room. Then say, "Jake, find Michelle," or whatever the person's name is. Now let go of the collar and see if your dog will go into the other room and to that person. It is okay to follow your dog. If he does go to the person, give your dog a C/T and a huge barnbuster reward along with praise.

**2.** Repeat five times and take a break.

**3.** After number two, have the family member go into different rooms, and do five repetitions in each room.

**4.** It will take a few sessions for your dog to learn and retain the names. Do not forget to reinforce practicing forever.

**Hands On**

I taught this to Jake, but my wife's Poodle Roxie knows many more names of objects, people, and places, but Jake can respectably perform all of the tricks in here. He is my pal and goes through all of these things willingly, but some days I have to give him a break, probably like crash test dummies in the car industry need a break.

Teaching Jake names while using the "touch" command I started out by using the touch command with my empty hand, and getting a peculiar look from him. He touched my hand and I C/T about a half dozen times. Holding Jakes attention while in the sitting position in front of me, I then I picked up the tug into my hand and repeated the exercise saying, "touch tug," and only C/T when he touched the tug. I'll confess it took a few attempts and me adjusting my hand so that he had to touch the tug when he moved his nose towards my hand holding the tug. I ran through exercises 1-4 over a few days and about six sessions.

Eventually, I felt confident to start moving the tug further from my body and then onto the floor, couch cushion, into the corner of the room and so forth. It took some time and patience for him to begin to understand right away to go to the item being named. Eventually, I was able to place it into different rooms inside the house and call out "touch tug" and he would bolt off looking for it. From there I added further toys such as Frisbee™, which I discovered by his ears and the way that he looked at me when I said the word that he already recognized the sound of the word.

## Troubleshooting

*I am scratching my head because my dog does not understand what I am trying to teach!*

In the beginning, you can try maneuvering your hand so that your dog will touch the toy and not your hand.

Watch your time when training. Keep your sessions short and if your dog is still a puppy or acting like one keep your sessions around 3-5 minutes, while older dogs can go about 10 minutes per training session. If you notice any signs of fatigue, end the session on a high, happy note, and stop for the day and begin anew the following day.

**Hint:** After your dog recognizes, and is regularly touching objects in different locations, solicit other people to practice giving your dog the command. Combine this with "take it" & "bring it" and your dog will go find and bring to you anything he has learned the name. Have fun and enjoy adding objects and names.


*...This book contains fun tricks as well as other useful tricks that all dogs should know that would benefit them and their owners. When your dog learns and masters all 49 ½ tricks, you will have a well-mannered, obedient, talented dog that is your friend, show-off, and companion. You two will be sure to get plenty of laughs and applause by combining these fun tricks and utilitarian commands.*

*I wrote this to help dog owners and trainers further their dog's abilities and the bond between dog and owner...*


### "49 ½ Dog Tricks"

**By Paul Allen Pearce**

## Will be available Soon

# 30  West Highland Terrier Facts

Country of Origin: Scotland

Other Names: Poltalloch Terrier, Roseneath Terrier, White Roseneath Terrier

Nicknames: Westie or Westy

Group: Terrier

Purpose: Rodent hunter

Size: Small

Height: Males 10 - 12 inches (25 - 30 cm) Females 9 - 11 inches (23 - 28 cm)

Weight: Males 15 - 22 pounds (7 - 10 kg) Females 13 - 16 pounds (6 - 7 kg)

Lifespan: 12-16 years

Litter Sizes: 3-5

Colors: White

Coat: Harsh double coat that requires regular brushing, trim around ears and eyes, trim coat around every four months, strip twice yearly.

Shedding: Little to none.

Apartment: Yes, extremely active indoors, can cope without a yard. Be sure properly to daily exercise.

Temperament: Confident, independent, some are good with children some are more aloof, social, friendly, strong prey drive, enjoy a good dig, good watchdog

Exercise: Long daily walks, fetch games with toys appeals to their prey drive.

Training: It is ranked 47th in Stanley Coren's "The Intelligence of Dogs" book, which statistically documents judge and trainer feedback on the top 100+ dogs. This translates into some Westies may need more repetitions than the other 47 popular dogs ahead of them, before learning and retaining commands or tricks. Their terriers and a bit stubborn, so firm, confident, consistent training will get you where you two need to go. Establish your alpha position and lead from there. The Westie needs this leadership to keep potential behavioral issues at bay. Treat them as you would a large dog.

# West Highland Terrier Rescue

West Highland Terriers are often acquired without any clear understanding of what goes into owning one, and these dogs regularly end up in the care of rescue groups, and are badly in need of adoption or fostering. If you are interested in adopting a Westie, a rescue group is a good place to start. I have listed a few below. If you have the facilities and ability please rescue a dog and enjoy the rewarding experience that it offers both of you.

*http://www.animalshelter.org/shelters/states.asp*

http://www.thekennelclub.org.uk/services/public/findarescue/Default.aspx ?breed=3082

http://www.westieclubamerica.com/rescue/

http://www.westierehoming.me.uk/about-us

# VISIT US TODAY!

**Share Our Links – Like us, Pin us, Feed it, Tweet it and Twerk it – We Need Help Too!**

**Please Comment** "Let us know what you think, did this book help you with training your dog, please take the time to REVIEW this guide and tell others about the positive information inside."

# Facebook.com/newdogtimes

# NewDogTimes.com

*"Thanks for reading. I hope you enjoyed this as much as I have enjoyed writing it and training my dog!"*

*"Keep on training and loving your Now Zen Like 'Kung-Fu' dog. Please be patient, loving, and have fun while training your dog."*

*~ Paul Allen Pearce*

## Think Like a Dog - but Don't Eat Your Poop!

**LEARN MORE**

amazon.com/dp/B00ICGQO40

# About the Author

Paul Allen Pearce is the author of many breed specific "Think Like a Dog" dog-training books.

As a youth, a family trip to Australia forever changed the course Paul would take on his way to return home to South Carolina to begin a family, raise dogs, and eventually write. For a year in high school, Paul headed back to Australia to study, and then again, during college he did the same. After finishing college, he headed to Africa to work with the Peace Corps.

Paul's family is dog lovers and often took in strays. Paul and his siblings were taught how to care and train the family pets and dogs. Both his parents grew up with many animals and had generational knowledge to pass forth to their offspring. Being reared around all sorts of animals, his curiosity to work with animals grew. Upon returning back to the U.S. and purchasing his own dog he realized he didn't know as much as he could, thus began his journey into owning and full time dog training.

Paul states, "Dog training is my passion. I love dogs, animals, and the wonders of nature. It is easy to write about your passion and share what you have learned and discovered. I hope that my readers enjoy and learn from what I have learned and improve their dog relationships. My past explorations throughout twenty countries and states helped me to broaden my perspective regarding animal behavior and treatment. Let us all be kind to animals, not only dogs."

**Facebook.com/newdogtimes**

# Other Books

**"Don't Think BE Alpha Dog Secrets Revealed"**

**"Puppy Training Stuff - The 14 Puppy Essentials**
*Your Puppy Needs Now"*

**"No Brainer Dog Trainer"**
**(Breed specific dog training series)**

# Content Attributions

**Photos:** We wish to thank all of the photographers for sharing their photographs via Creative Commons Licensing.

COVER https://upload.wikimedia.org/wikipedia/commons/1/17/Westie_pups.jpg, By Lucie Tylová, Westik.cz (Westieinfo.com - soukromý archiv) [GFDL (http://www.gnu.org/copyleft/fdl.html) or CC BY-SA 3.0 (http://creativecommons.org/licenses/by-sa/3.0)], via Wikimedia Commons, no changes made

BIO1 https://www.flickr.com/photos/a4gpa/864629505/, CC License 2.0 ShareAlike https://creativecommons.org/licenses/by-sa/2.0/legalcodc, Bailey, By a4gpa, no changes made.

BIO2 https://www.flickr.com/photos/randysonofrobert/289028932, CC License 2.0 Generic https://creativecommons.org/licenses/by/2.0/legalcode, Wee Westie on the California Sand, By Randy Robertson, no changes made

NAME https://upload.wikimedia.org/wikipedia/commons/1/17/Westie_pups.jpg, By Lucie Tylová, Westik.cz (Westieinfo.com - soukromý archiv) [GFDL (http://www.gnu.org/copyleft/fdl.html) or CC BY-SA 3.0 (http://creativecommons.org/licenses/by-sa/3.0)], via Wikimedia Commons, no changes made

TRAINING https://www.flickr.com/photos/randysonofrobert/295843069, CC License 2.0 Generic https://creativecommons.org/licenses/by/2.0/legalcode, Wee Westie, By Randy Robertson, no changes made

CLICKER https://www.flickr.com/photos/potirons/13946707487/, P1360641 (2), By Denis789, cropped all four side removing frame

TERRIER TRAITS https://pixabay.com/en/dog-west-white-white-dog-pride-1180858/

TERRIER TRAITS2 https://upload.wikimedia.org/wikipedia/commons/6/66/Westhighlandterrier-jumping.jpg, By Chri stian H. (Own work) [Public domain], via Wikimedia Commons, no changes made

SIT https://www.flickr.com/photos/bluetigger/170372815, CC License 2.0 Generic https://creativecommons.org/licenses/by/2.0/legalcode, Sitting in the grass, By olaszemelo, cropped left side

DOWN https://pixabay.com/en/west-highland-white-terrier-westie-76286/